Love and Law

Also by Ernest Holmes

Love and Law

The Unpublished Teachings

Ernest Holmes

Edited by Marilyn Leo

Jeremy P. Tarcher/Penguin
a member of Penguin Group (USA) Inc.
New York

Jeremy P. Tarcher/Penguin
a member of
Penguin Group (USA) Inc.
375 Hudson Street
New York, NY 10014
www.penguin.com

First trade paperback edition 2004
Copyright © 2001 by United Church of Religious Science
All rights reserved. This book, or parts thereof, may not
be reproduced in any form without permission.
Published simultaneously in Canada

The Library of Congress catalogued the hardcover
edition as follows:

Holmes, Ernest, 1887–1960.
Love and law : the unpublished teachings / Ernest Holmes ;
edited by Marilyn Leo.
p.   cm.
ISBN 1-58542-077-8
1. United Church of Religious Science—Doctrines.
2. Spiritual life—United Church of Religious Science.
I. Leo, Marilyn.   II. Title.
BP605.U53 H64   2001   00-062921
299'.93—dc21
ISBN 1-58542-302-5 (Paperback edition)

Printed in the United States of America
1   3   5   7   9   10   8   6   4   2

Book design by Meighan Cavanaugh

Contents

Part I
Fundamentals of Metaphysics—September 1918

Part II
Tuesday and Thursday Lectures— September/October 1918

Part III
A Series of Private Lessons — 1918–1920

About This Book

Yellowed and brittle, the pages of transcription by students of Ernest Holmes now, once again through this book, bring to life words to live by. There is a message of depth to show us how we may choose a life that can be more beneficial for us and the world. This book is prepared in three parts. It consists of three different series of talks given around the same time, 1918. Ernest was known to give a morning lecture, a different lecture in the afternoon, and perhaps an evening class, all in the same day.

Ernest, as he was usually addressed, never prepared his lectures with notes or manuscript. He lived in the Presence of God, and his profound ideas come to prove this. We must take into account the era of these lectures. World War I ended in November 1918, and this war is referred to in some of his lectures. Also at this time there was a major epidemic of influenza in Europe and America.

Ernest had an amazing memory for literature, poetry, and the Bible. However, many Bible quotes are not word for word. He studied the King James Version, and the verses he refers to may be found there. At times it seems he created his own words. You will also find a few slang terms of the day. The editor has, where necessary, brought gender inclusiveness to the lectures. In a few cases there were words left out by the stenographer; these additions have been made.

Throughout the years people have asked if Ernest Holmes believed and spoke the same in his early years, around 1916, as in his last, 1960. I would have to say yes and no. What he believed about our choice and how we create our own world remained the same. How he expressed his beliefs may have mellowed a bit in later years. His first book, *Creative Mind*, is about these beliefs in clear and concise terms. His last book, *The Voice Celestial*, coauthored with his brother Fenwicke Holmes, is an entirely different kind of book: a book of poetry.

Ernest was very much the mystic. In a talk he gave in 1958 in Whittier, California, he comes to a place where he believes he has seen "the veil, and it is very thin."

Sometimes people have felt that Ernest spoke and emphasized the Law rather than Love. But he believed that "Love points the way and the Law makes the thing possible." The thing being the desire manifested. In one of his lectures on Fundamental Metaphysics he states: "You will find your word has the amount of power, the amount of intelligence you put into it, and it has creative power according to the amount of absolute conviction and the impulse of love which is behind it."

The use of the term *practitioner* was gleaned by Ernest's early exposure to Christian Science. A practitioner is a person who practices the principles of Science of Mind. There are now people who have studied and been licensed through the organization of the United Church of Religious Science as professional practitioners. In 1920 there were only a couple of people in this position. They were Reginald Armor and Anna Holmes, Ernest's mother. The practitioners and patients that Ernest is referring to throughout his talks are the people he was speaking to, not licensed practitioners.

"There is no practitioner that can do anything more for you than to help you. Your final emancipation will be written by your own hand or it will never be written at all, it will be thought out by your own mind. It will govern your own consciousness as it recognizes the supremacy of mind, the infinite impulse of spirit, and your own divine birthright to use it." In other words, the final determination of your healing is up to you, in your acceptance of truth. As Jesus said: "It is done unto you *as* you believe."

Editor

Rev. Marilyn [Armor] Leo

About the Author

Ernest Shurtleff Holmes, public speaker, religious leader, and author, was born in Lincoln, Maine, on January 21, 1887, one of nine sons of William Nelson, a farmer, and Anna Columbia (Heath) Holmes.

Ernest received his education in the rural schools of his native community, the public schools of Lincoln, Maine, and Gould's Academy, in Bethel, Maine. From 1908 to 1910 he attended the Leland Powers School of Expression, in Boston, while at the same time working in a retail store, which he continued to do for the next three years.

In 1912 he went to California, where he served as playground instructor and purchasing agent for the City of Venice. Beginning about 1915, he was asked to speak in a friend's home about his beliefs and philosophy. He quickly grew in popularity and until the early 1960s he was prolific in his lectures as well as successful at publishing books. By 1916 he began lecturing in auditoriums in Los Angeles to many hundreds of people.

He and his brother Fenwicke established a home in Venice,

California, for metaphysical treatment. In 1916 they also began publishing a magazine, *The Uplift*. In 1917 they organized the Southern California Metaphysical Institute and in 1918 established a metaphysical sanitarium in Long Beach.

During these few years Ernest maintained a lecture hall and treatment offices in Los Angeles and spoke on Sundays in the Strand Theater. In 1920, he and his brother traveled to New York, Boston, and Philadelphia, where they spoke to overflow crowds in lecture halls and theaters. Finally, in the early 1920s, Ernest sought more permanency and stability in his endeavors by confining his work primarily to one location. He then returned to Los Angeles and began to steadily expand his career, lecturing in the Biltmore and Ambassador Hotels. He established headquarters in the North Parlor of the Trinity Hotel (later known as the Embassy), conducting midweek meetings and special classes. Ernest's mother and his lifelong friend Reginald Armor established offices in this location as practitioners to meet the needs of the ever-increasing number of followers.

In 1927 he founded the Institute of Religious Science and School of Philosophy, which was later changed to the Church of Religious Science and, most recently, the United Church of Religious Science. He served as dean of the school and leader of the church organization until the close of his life. Also in 1927, on October 23, Ernest was married in Los Angeles to Hazel Foster, daughter of Charles and Ann Durkee. They had no children.

Ernest had a casual form. He often wore plaid shirts and loafer shoes and was completely comfortable with whomever he was with, whether celebrities of Hollywood, university professors, or the indigent. He was at home in his surroundings. The feeling behind some of these lectures of sitting in his living room with a roaring fire is accurate. He, along with his beloved wife, Hazel, celebrated life often in their home with many friends. There was most often conversation, with Ernest asking questions of others as well as giving his own personal views about life, the universe, and how it all works.

The same year (1927) he founded a monthly magazine, *Religious Science*, which later became *Science of Mind*. Ernest was editorial director. This magazine has gained worldwide recognition and distribution.

At the time of his death in Los Angeles on April 7, 1960, the number of branch church organizations had risen to 101, in all parts of the world, most of these housed in their own buildings and with a registered membership exceeding 100,000. He lived to dedicate the Founder's Church in Los Angeles in January 1960. It is a magnificent edifice, costing more than $1,500,000. Its minister was Dr. William H. D. Hornaday.

Ernest lectured incessantly, and his published writings are prolific. His central thesis was his own definition of Religious Science in less than twenty-five words as "a correlation of the laws of science, opinions of philosophy, and revelations of religion applied to human needs and the aspirations of all." He took the transcendental position of accepting a First Cause, although he supported his thesis with logical arguments derived from the sciences and the authority of the outstanding thinkers of history, formulating a basic synchronism which he taught as a system of religion. He accepted the principle of idealistic monism and declared that science and religion are rooted in one and the same Mind, and that the world of phenomena is subject to the Law of Mind. He considered that people are an individualization of Creative Spirit and through their self-awareness and power of choice can control the health of the body and the conditions of environment by affirmative meditation, which he called treatment. To this end he maintained the necessity of understanding the principle of the Law of Mind, which responds automatically to any demand made upon it. Successful, wise, and affirmative employment of this Law result in what we call "good," and an unwise or negative use of this law will result in so-called evil. Evil is therefore an effect and not a cause. He quoted the Bible often: "It is not the will of my Father that any of his children should perish." He believed that the final answer lies in the receptivity of the individual: "Ask and ye shall receive."

Ernest was an eloquent speaker and wrote widely in the fields of the new psychology, spiritual philosophy, and metaphysics. His consuming passion was to teach teachers. His counsel and assistance were sought by many noted people across the country. Thousands flocked to his classes.

Some of his books are:

Creative Mind, 1919

Creative Mind and Success, 1919

Science of Mind, 1926 (revised edition 1938—known as the "text book")

The Bible in the Light of Religious Science, 1929

Ebell Lectures on Spiritual Science, 1934

It's Up to You, 1936

Your Invisible Power, 1940

Mind Remakes Your World, (editor), 1941

New Thought Terms and Their Meanings, 1942

This Thing Called Life, 1943

This Thing Called You, 1948

How to Use the Science of Mind, 1948

Words That Heal Today, 1949

You Will Live Forever, 1960

Among the books that he coauthored are:

Values, with Milton Sills, 1932

Questions and Answers on the Science of Mind, with Alberta Smith, 1935

Help for Today, with William H. D. Hornaday, 1958

A New Design for Living, with Willis Kinnear, 1959

The Voice Celestial, with Fenwicke Holmes, 1960

Ernest received many honorary degrees. Among them: Litt. D. degree in 1947 from Western University, Bengal, India; and Ph.D. in 1945 from Andhra Research University, India. He was also made a Fellow, L.H.D., in 1945 of the College of Osteopathic Physicians and Surgeons of Los Angeles, now named the California Medical College of Osteopathic Physicians and Surgeons.; Litt. D. in 1949 from the Foundation Academic University of Spiritual Understanding, Venice, Italy; Diploma of Honor in 1948 from the Institute of Neapolitan Culture, Naples, Italy; and honorary Diploma of Vidya Ratna in 1948 from the Gondal Rashala Asuhadhashram, Gondal, Kalhiawad, India. In 1942 he was named Commander of the Cross by the Association of the Humanitarian Grand Prize of Belgium, and in 1944 was named honorary member of the Eugene Field Society, a national group of authors and journalists. In 1950 he was given the Freedom Foundation award.

Additional information on the life of Ernest Holmes may be found in the following books:

Armor, Reginald C. *That Was Ernest.* DeVorss (Los Angeles, CA) 1999

Armor, Reginald C. *Ernest Holmes the Man.* Science of Mind Publications (Los Angeles, CA) 1977

About the Author

Holmes, Fenwicke. *Ernest Holmes, His Life & Times.* Dodd Mead (New York) 1970

Hornaday, William H. D. *Your Alladin's Lamp.* Science of Mind Publications (Los Angeles, CA) 1979, formerly published as *The Inner Light.* Dodd Mead (New York) 1964

Vahle, Neal *Open at the Top.* Open View Press (Marin Co., CA) 1993

Part I

Fundamentals of Metaphysics

A series of Monday Evening Lectures
September 1918
Los Angeles, California

Mind Your Own Business

There is only one thing that I ask of you and that is that you will believe absolutely that this thing works. If you do not believe it works it will not work, because everything is belief. Everything is mind and all operation is thought, and there is not a law in the universe that is not the power of mind in action and there never was and there never will be. Anything you ever saw or ever will see is simply the result of mind in action. You have a body and you have what we call a physical environment, and you would have neither if it were not for mind. When mind desires your body to disappear, your body will disappear. What the re-embodiment will be nobody does know. If you can learn to live today and get a lot out of life, and have as much fun as I have had today, and be as prosperous as we all ought to be, and be well, you should not worry what is going to happen tomorrow. You take absolutely too much responsibility upon yourself. It amounts to fear, which is a natural consequence of the belief in limitation.

I want to endeavor to show you how you can become less limited. I say again, this will mean absolutely nothing to you, it is

worthless, useless, unless you absolutely believe it, and not only believe it but that you go right at it as though you had always known
it and it had always worked and there was no possibility of failure.
You will get the biggest results if you will say nothing to anybody
of what you want to do. If we could add to the commandments,
the greatest would be *mind your own business.*

The law implanted within mind by an all-wise, all-intelligent
Creator is that you need nothing but yourself and an all-wise, all-
powerful Creator to produce anything. And just as far as you believe your success and all possibilities of life depend upon any
condition or person, past, present or future, you are creating chaos,
and that because of your own false thought. That is the absolute
truth. You have this infinite mental principle.

Tonight I want you to consider yourselves as the infinite or
creative power—mind. For your purpose now I want you to consider it as mind which is latent, ready to manifest, lying dormant.
Of course, it is not; everything in the universe is activity. I want
you to think of it as mind ready to receive an impression and
spring into activity. If you say that to many metaphysicians—
Christian Scientists, for instance—they will say it is mortal mind,
the activity of God in expression.

Every living soul is a law unto himself, but of this most people
are unconscious. Now, there is no sentiment to this. You could not
sit down in that chair and by declaring that God is good bring
prosperity to you. Of course, God is good but everything is good.

Realize that we are dealing with an eternal principle which is
mathematically correct. I notice this, that it is not to the sentimen-
tal ones who gush and gush, that big results come, it is to those
who think deeply and simply and pertinently and persistently, and
then, because they know. In what they believe, they know they will
get a perfect result. This is the sum and substance of the whole

thing, for you can then approach the Infinite Mind with a depth of understanding and thought, with a realization that you are dealing with reality, with a tremendous reverence that so far transcends the orthodox idea of prayer that you can compare them only as you can compare this planet with a mole hill. With the utmost reverence we worship that Being we call God. What the person of this God is no person knows or ever has known, but what the activity of this principle is we do know. Its greatest activity is through the human instrument. We say we are the activity of God in expression; that there is one power, infinite, operating, always producing, eternally creating, and flowing through you and all at the level of your consciousness. Now, I have no doubt but that is the truth.

In this mind we seem to be a three-fold activity. Of course, we do not have three minds; we have only one mind. But for the sake of clear thinking, we seem to be objective, subjective and spiritual.

The Word speaks and the word becomes a law and the law manifests conditions. And so we speak forth into this Mind, this infinite, creative power, and it returns to us; so it seems and so it absolutely does.

There is something, and believe me it is not something to be lightly dealt with—there is something that casts back at you manifested every word you speak. "Vengeance is mine," saith the Lord, "I will repay." This is a statement of eternal correspondences against which nothing can stand. And whatever you set in motion in this eternal mind, it will be done unto you even as you have conceived within yourself and brought forth from thought into manifestation.

The trouble with us, why we are poor and sick and miserable, is what I want to speak about. Right off I want to begin to talk about the demonstration of conditions. You see, when we are dealing with this thing, we are dealing with nothing we can bring to please any living soul. It is truth. It is absolute. It is exacting. It is the law of cause and effect. And don't think it is anything else. Now, to that you may add all the sentiment you want to, and it is good. Sometimes I cry as I talk, I feel so big inside. To think that great intelligence is operating through me. Without that definite clear-thinking intelligence behind it, it would be nothing but a mess of mush and we could not work with it. The universe is run by intelligence, and the trouble is we have separated ourselves from that intelligence upon which the universe is run, and that is all the trouble.

There is a mind which does not know you and me as Ernest Holmes and Mary Jones and John Smith. It knows that it is, and it knows that everything it receives it creates. Let us consider this universal mind and find some names for it. You are surrounded by universal mind which is receptive. It receives the slightest impress of your thought. It is neutral, it receives any thought. Did you ever stop to consider the wind will sail a boat whichever way you set the rudder and tack. All mind is receptive, ready to act when acted upon. It is creative. It creates wherever it wants to. It is absolutely impersonal. Once in Samuel and once in Psalms it says, speaking of this universal mind, this law of cause and effect, *It is done unto you as you believe.* It means it will become to us what we believe. It is impersonal, impartial, receptive, creative, conscious. It is infinitely creative, your consciousness and my consciousness. It is called the great feminine. In the esoteric literature there is the masculine and the feminine—the active and the passive. In our Bible, "In the beginning there was God" and "the Spirit moved upon the water." Water, esoterically speaking, means spirit. In baptizing, people in some traditions are immersed in water to symbolize the fact that they are immersed in the spirit. It is the general teaching that the Infinite One is both active and passive, masculine and feminine. This is of no practical value to you or to me, but it is so.

Spirit moves upon spirit and produces an infinite substance from which it shall operate and manifest this body. Whether or not that is true I do not know, but everything happens just as though it were true. We know we have a creative mind within us which will receive the impress of our thought and build our body. Our creative mind is our share of the universal creative mind; and whatever is true about you is universally true, whatever is universally true must also be true about you. Now, this mind is infinite intelligence, infinite creative power, receptivity, and all the other things I have just named it. Now, this mind receives the impress of our thought like the soil received a seed and reproduces it.

Here is a great thing, a lesson to learn—it is one, it is self-conscious all over. That means a great deal—the unity of mind. It means this, that when you and I speak, our word goes to a point in mind; that it is neither beyond the point nor approaching it—there has been brought to bear infinite intelligence at the point. I have, then, all the creative power in the universe, poured through my word. And sometimes, under the right conditions, in spite of all our belief we are almost frightened by the rapidity with which this thing works.

It is eternally seeking avenues of expression. That is what we call the divine urge. It is the need which makes the butterfly burst forth. It is what makes the seed break open a stone wall to express as a plant. It is the thing that makes me teach metaphysics. There is something that will express wherever there is any possibility of an avenue of expression, but if we will get out of the way and let it express, wonderful things will happen, but according to natural law. No law is broken. The great thing, remember, is this—you are thinking all the time. You cannot stop thinking, there is no living soul can stop thinking one second, day or night, throughout all eternity. It is the activity of mind. You are, then, always stirring up this cosmic mind and causing it to do something. Now, we generally do it in ignorance, but ignorance of the law excuses nobody.

We are learning to constantly control our thought so we can perfectly control our conditions. It embodies everything. The universe is so big we think that mind reaches out and out into infinity. As infinite as that mind is it is in you, and it is nowhere else that the demonstration takes place. It is your mind. It is all the mind you have got, only we do not know it. We have separated it, and it is because of our divine individuality we have had the power to separate it. This is the answer to the problem of evil and good.

We say, if it is true that God is good and God wants us to have everything that is good, why does God create us and let us suffer? Why are we limited? Why must we struggle, struggle against physical limitations? And here is the answer as it appears to me. I believe it is true. It is like this. We are individuals. To be an individual must always be to have the right of self-choice. Had God created us to be mechanical, we would not have been an individual. The planet is mechanical, it has got to be what it is, it cannot move out of its course, but we can. God could not make a mechanical individual. That is an absolute impossibility and since God could not make us so we had to go one way, God had to make us and let us go the way we saw fit. And if you will think that out it will answer all of the problem of evil.

We are what we are because of ignorance. "I set before you the curse and the blessing. Choose you this day whom you shall serve." Jesus saw the law of cause and effect. He said, "It is done unto you as you believe." and "Judge not that ye be not judged, for with what judgment you judge you shall be judged." Jesus saw both the law and through it. He drew the veil. And what gave Jesus the power to become the Christ was that he, himself, had lifted the veil of Isis and had seen the Father-Mother God face-to-face revealed there as one soul, and speaking from his own soul, said, "The Father and I are one."

The same mind that is in us is in the universe, the same mind, no difference. Now then, we reflect into this Universal Mind what we think. Practically the whole human race is hypnotized because it thinks what somebody else told it to think. It thinks from its physical environment. It says, I see sin, sickness, death, misery, unhappiness, I see calamity, and so it is giving to the creative, receptive, impersonal, eternal mind a concept, it is giving a law. Do you know what law means? It does not care if it slays you. If people would wake up and realize that law is law and not think they can say twiddle diddle dee and change law. You cannot change law. And Jesus was the first scientific man that ever lived because he saw the law as it was.

This impersonal, eternal law receives the impression of my thought and if I say, "Everything is wrong," it is wrong. In Christian Science they call it the law of reflection. Like produces like; like attracts like; like draws to itself like, always.

If you could see your thought and take a picture of it and of your conditions, you would see no difference between them. We cannot make affirmations and denials for fifteen minutes and spend the other twenty-three hours and forty-five minutes denying the thing we have affirmed and affirming the thing we have denied and obtain the results we seek.

We send out the word and it sets in motion the power, but if we begin to think the opposite thing, it gets the word as soon as it is thought. It neutralizes the word and destroys any possibility of its effect.

I have to sort of hurl these things out, for I have not time to go into them. You will have to do that yourselves.

You cannot demonstrate one iota beyond your mental ability to conceive.

Nothing is impossible to It but I am an individual and at the very doorway of my consciousness It must stand and wait. "Behold, I stand at the door and knock." I have to open it. The knocking is mental.

You will never demonstrate as long as you deal with a condition. We live in Mind. Mind is fluent. That is why Jesus could pass right through a solid wall.

As infinite as that creative principle is, as receptive and quick, it can only become to the individual what the individual can conceive. This is one of the great truths of metaphysics—God can become to the individual only what God can become through the individual. The law of belief again. I have to have something in me to correspond. It is infinite, but I have to provide a seed—a mental equivalent, and my demonstration will equal the equivalent, or seed of thought, which is implanted in the Universal Mind which takes it up—which is the immaculate conception—it is within itself, out of itself, and out of itself preceding itself into the manifestation always. That is the process of involution which always comes before evolution—the going into and the coming out of or from. Involution is the activity of the spirit upon itself. All manifestation is the activity of the spirit upon itself. In practical experience, it means this—I have created for me, or produced, only that which is first within me. Now, is not that an awful thing? Since it is that way we have got to provide the necessary condition. Jesus said, "When ye pray believe that ye have and ye shall receive." Believe that ye have, that it is now a positive thing done, and so receive. That will set the law in motion and Divine order will produce the thing.

Suppose I wanted a home. There are certain brands of people who do not believe in demonstrating things, but that is for each one of us to work out for ourselves. Jesus, who certainly was wise, and good, and powerful, and truthful to principle—so true that he died for it—did not hesitate to even turn water into wine because the people happened to want it. If I were asked, would you use a spiritual means to produce a physical thing my reply would be, there is nothing but Spirit. Your body is spiritual. There is nothing but Spirit. The fact that we have believed it to be something that it is not, you cannot change Universal Mind, you can only change your thought. That is enough. Scientifically set in motion, the law will bring the thing you want.

We must do as it is written, but we write it ourselves. We write out the figure on the wall with a cosmic hand, the cosmic hand passes on but the law becomes eternal because the mind recognizes it is infinite all at once.

I must have a perfect concept of what I want. I must accept the fact that I have got it. Insofar as I look to see where it is coming from I will not get it, because I will then be doubting it. It is a fear and a doubt which neutralizes the positive effort. Jesus said, "When ye pray believe that ye have received." Before you speak, God answers. The minute I think, it is universal because of the unity of Mind. There is a reason for everything in this world if we could only read the reason. It is the law of our own true nature that binds us on the wheel which eternally turns. Get a mental equivalent.

A practitioner gives the same treatment for each one. The law of correspondences, that is, the mental likeness they have got. They believe as they believe because that is all they could believe, their consciousness is not expanded to get more. A marvelous truth, we have to get a greater thing within. That is why Jesus said, "Seek ye first the kingdom of heaven." So, you see, we each draw to our self that which we are and that which we believe, and, because Jesus had a concept of the infinite, of good, of the omnipotence, of the omniscience and of the omnipresence of the Spirit within him, is it any wonder he could do the things he did? That he could manifest loaves and fishes to feed five thousand, manifest them right out of the air. It is being done in a commercial way today and the time will come when everything will be done right out of the air.

The beginning is in Mind, and the time will come when the florist will find the flower before the seed. That should mean something to you. This is the secret of life; it is the secret of success. It is the secret of demonstration, and believe me, the waiting world needs that you shall demonstrate. "I, if I be lifted up and not dragged down, shall draw the world unto me." It is your solemn duty to yourself, to society, to the human race that you demonstrate the absolute power of spiritual thought over all so-called physical resistance.

I have given you just a suggestion of the way the law works—law! Law! *Law!* The one who knows it most gets the best results. To us who can understand the law, the law is understanding, is spiritual realization. That person is a well-rounded metaphysician and will get what is desired and will never fail. We are not only using an infinite law but that something which made the law.

Law is an effect—wonderful as law is—the word came first. The word had to come before the law, and the law is but the word in action. You are a law unto yourself. Know the spirit behind the law and so use the law. It is a fact that just to use this law mentally might bring upon us calamity. That is, to get to using this law for selfish ends there is a law which does just as I tell you it does. The spirit of Christ is in the individual who perceives this law and uses it from the standpoint of the creative spirit, who speaks it forth for the unfoldment of the human race. The spirit of Christ within

12

is realized by the one who is continually working in union with the Father.

The spirit of anti-Christ is the one who sees simply the law and not the spirit behind it and uses it for selfish gains and to control conditions.

Every living soul has to settle their own questions of life. We are endowed with ability to think and choose and do what we want to do. But I believe that in as far as you use universal law for unfoldment and a greater degree of livingness for yourself or for the human race, which in no way contends against anybody else's mind, which in no way seeks to control anybody else's mind, but operating directly from cause to effect, from Spirit which is substance into manifestation, which is nature, you have that right whether it is for yourself or for anyone else. There is a power which backs up your word which nothing can withstand.

To handle it in business: There is just as much power in a treatment as you put into it. The word which you speak seems to be endowed with a creative power of its own. That word may manifest after hundreds of years with power.

The most important thing here is the way to give a treatment. Realize it is not I who is speaking but the spirit of Christ within me, the only begotten Son of God. I dissolve first the thought of my personality, then I dissolve the thought of personality from the one I desire to help. I realize the unity of God: There is one God, there is one spirit, there is one law, there is one cause, there is one effect, there is but one body. If you knew there was one body and it is God, you would never be sick again. You are a member of that body.

There is but one law; that law is eternal action, *eternal action*. We should realize that it is always doing something. I would declare that this so-called law of inactivity has nothing to stand upon. It is not law, it is a myth, it is a hypnotic state of carnal thought, carnal belief.

This word which I speak knows itself to be the only power there is. It knows itself to be the law of annihilation, and elimination. I should declare there is one activity here present in my condition, in my affairs, there is one attraction. I am the spirit of attraction within thee, that one divine attraction which unites its ideas with everything.

Then, I should get the most perfect concept of the thing I desired and then and there I should go forth and do. I should believe in it as I had never believed in anything since I was born. It knows itself to be that which it is. It is not my word, but it knows itself to be God's word, and that makes it go forth with power and nothing can hinder it. You state that it will exist eternally and it will never cease.

Then you wait. Perfect passivity. It is now done. The law is perfectly operative. Do not be passive like a sponge. Never, as long as you live, try to concentrate.

Suppose I have made my treatment, I have declared the truth, and say I want to attract a lot of activity. I would take this statement, *I am the eternal law of attraction within thee.* I would begin to let those words float before me. Other thoughts would come and I would not try to get rid of them, I am just thinking those words, I would not pay any attention to the other thoughts. Then think it more and more and more. It will always be attracting. It is the law of life. It is true because it is true. I should realize that until there was such a sense of peace and calm expectance and trust that I would just feel and know it is done. I should do it until it manifested. You have got to break down every so-called law of matter and limitation that exists in your consciousness. You have got to work and you will get absolutely nothing until you do.

There is a perfect concept and you have got to bring it forth.

But, believe me, behind the treatment don't deny your Lord. I am not sick, I am not weak, I am not poor. *I am not sick, I am not weak, I am not poor. I am that I am, and beside me there is none other. From everlasting I speak, and none can stay my voice. It is done.*

> *The sun across its course may go,*
> *The ancient rivers still may flow,*
> *I am and still I am.*

If you could realize the infinite light, the majestic power, if you could realize something of that mind which holds within itself all the great system of planets and says to every one, "Thus far and no more," and it is done; if you could realize the tremendous power of attraction that holds everything in its place, it is yours, it is yours, this gift. It is the divine birthright of every living soul, but we limit ourselves by thought of limitation. Now, we must open up the doors of our consciousness and expand and expand and expand, and no longer think in the terms of the backyard lot but in the terms of the infinite nature, in the terms of the universe.

When Earth's last picture is painted, eternal, majestic, infinite mind flowing through your soul, it is perfect, it is complete. It is cause, it is effect, it is conditions, it is creative power. *It is all.* Take it!

The Power
Is in Your Word

I have long wanted to experiment, to take a group of people and see if we could not get some results in demonstrating, as we get with one person. I am daily getting letters and telephone messages from people who have been healed through our class work. I do not see any reason, since the principle of Mind is infinite, why we could not make one treatment just as effective for one hundred and fifty people as for one, provided those one hundred and fifty people receive it. I am convinced that this thing will work with the same assurance as in an individual case, through the consciousness, and in the affairs of as many people as believe in it. There is something that corresponds with our every belief no matter what that belief is.

Now, the reason why so few people get from the metaphysical principle what there is in it is because, and it is a tragedy too, and it is a shame, so few people compared with the number of people there are in the world will take the time to learn to investigate and to understand. Ordinary people are so bound up with their trouble and fears and ignorance, they will not give the time it takes to change their thought. It is only normal and natural from the human standpoint that it should be so. Until your thought is changed your conditions never will be, your body never will be. We are sick because in our consciousness there is an image of disease. We will be sick just as long as that image exists. We are poor because of the same reason. There is not any question about it whatever, not the slightest. We externalize every concept and every consciousness and every state of mind. Now, it depends upon the individuals who are being helped just as much as it does the ones who are helping. For instance, in the infinity of Mind, which is the principle of all metaphysics and of all life, there is nothing but Mind and that which Mind does. That is all there is in the universe. That is all there ever was or ever will be. This Mind is latent. It just waits to be acted upon. And your thought and mind act upon Universal Mind. Your thought and my thought is a law unto ourselves. It is just as much a law unto your life and mine as God's law is in the universe. There is no difference. It is absolute, and moreover all there is in your life and mine is our thought, or our word, or its activity. Nothing can hinder it from manifesting. So receptive, so plastic, so quick to take an impression is this mentality which surrounds us that it receives the impress of our slightest thought.

Now, for the sake of clearness, I want you to think of yourself as in this Mind. Don't think of this Mind as being in you; rather think of yourself as a center in this Mind. Of course, this mind flows through you, but think of yourself as a center in it. That is your principle. You think and this Mind produces it. Now there is one of the big points in metaphysics and it is one of the reasons why so few people succeed. They do not understand the impersonal nature of Mind. They think, "I've got something tremendous to do, I have to hold the thought." Thinking the thought is what does something. Thought sows the seed in Mind, and without this Mind nothing could be made. You could not be sick without it. It is not your mind, so no human thought has anything to do with it. It is Mind, infinite and changeless, eternal, and all the mind there is. It will give us an entirely different concept of the metaphysical principle if, instead of thinking my mind does so and so, we think Mind does it. Of course, it is your mind; also, it is your principle.

That person gets the best results who realizes the impersonality of Mind, the absoluteness of it, and then who can project into it the clearest concept. The reason being that all is a law of cause and effect. We think a thought into Mind and Mind returns it to us manifested as we thought it. First, the impulse to think, then the thought, then the thought is imaged in infinite Mind, and infinite Mind creates and causes it to become an effect. That is always the way it works. Just see how we may relieve ourselves! The responsibility rests in Mind to do the creating, and not in you and not in me. We are not responsible for the slightest thing in this regard. What I mean is this: Neither by your taking thought or by my taking thought, humanly thinking, could we do the slightest thing. But there is the principle that flows in and through us and everybody that does the thing. That means that in your work you can be absolutely impersonal. If I were treating myself, as I do sometimes, I would not say, "I am so and so"; I call my name and treat myself as somebody I never heard of, because Mind is impersonal and Mind takes up this thought about Ernest Holmes and does it for me. Don't you see how, if you can get that concept, it is going to relieve you of all burden that the ordinary individual feels?

Suppose you sit down to give a treatment today at eight o'clock, we will say, and at eight-thirty another, and at nine o'clock you give another. It is the same treatment that is given each time. You see, you speak forth and Mind takes up what you say and does it unto you. That is why Jesus said, "It shall be done unto you . . . done *unto* you." And if you could relieve your own human consciousness of responsibility, you would be a good healer.

It is hard to speak forth and let it go away from you. "I will send forth my word and it shall not return to me void." We have got to learn to trust this unseen power. Until we do, we will get no results.

In this Mind there is held and flows the consciousness of the human race. Never forget that! It is one of the things that few people understand, that we are surrounded by a universal consciousness which is creative. And do you remember that I said it is receptive and neutral? It holds within itself all the thoughts of everybody, every thought that has been thought always by the human race, and it holds it and executes it.

There has been a thought gone forth into the human race that we are lost. It is perhaps one of the strongest thoughts that has ever been created, that we have fallen. That has become a very great mental suggestion operating on what we might term the universal cosmic plane, operating with terrific power through the consciousness of everybody who believes it. We are not talking about God, we are talking about our creative mind. It is a law, that is all. The very fact that it is not limited intelligence is shown in that it will receive both positive and negative impressions. Never get away from the idea that you are surrounded by such a power. It is the principle of demonstration. It knows everything. As we send forth our thought into it, it does it unto us. But that person who does not know how to deal with the metaphysical principle is bound by the law of human ignorance, absolutely bound hand and foot by conditions.

But, now, what does a metaphysician do? We begin, one by one, to break the chains of human consciousness which bind us. It is absolutely necessary. There is operative through the consciousness of the individual that law which says the person is sick, and is subject to being sick. We have got to absolutely break it and emancipate ourselves from it. How are you going to do it? You are going to do it by the same means that brought about the condition, by thinking, because everything is produced by thought. You are going to do it by thinking into Universal Mind the truth about yourself. The highest truth is that we are power, spirit, substance. We are made in the image of God; we are perfect.

Now, then, your treatment has just exactly as much, and no more power than you put into it. Can you understand that, since this is the mental principle of everything that is, it has got to accept our word. Do you get the fact that you are a mental being living in a mental universe? It is all right, it is real, but it is an effect, it is not a cause.

Here is one thing that you must think. It is one of the most important things. Since all is Mind and the only avenue of expression of this Mind is through mental concept, and we are the ones that hold the mental concept about ourselves, and Mind is the one which does it unto us—that mental concept held in Universal Mind is positive or negative as it is when we create it or think it. In other words, if I know that my word is, my word knows that it is. I say a treatment has no more power than is put into it by the one treating. And that is why some people's work is so much more powerful than others'. In some things I get much better results than I do in other things. There are certain things I can do for myself and never fail. Why? Because I know when I speak the word, that word knows itself. How, why do I know? Because somehow or other there is evolved within me that consciousness. That is a matter of growth. Notwithstanding, no treatment will have any more power than I put into it.

And here is an important thing, and it is a thing all the best metaphysicians understand, and the vast majority who are seeking do not: When you give your treatment you must know within your own consciousness that this treatment is the activity of absolute intelligence, absolute power, and that it knows within itself. That is why Mind knows this treatment is eternal, it cannot be upset, it cannot be waylaid, it cannot be operated against. Ordinary people's treatment does not go forth with power because their treatment is not protected in their mind. I am getting into deep waters, but I want you to follow me closely. Their treatment is not protected in their consciousness. We are dealing with a power where a positive and negative power balance each other. Until our word becomes so absolutely spiritual, it is very apt to be neutralized by an opposing power insofar as the effect on us is concerned. Since that is true, suppose you are demonstrating prosperity; you must do more than declare you are prosperous. You must know that no human law, no human thought, which is always seeking manifestation, can operate against your treatment. It knows itself to be the fulfillment of everything concerning you, and you will then surround yourself with a wall and protection of positive thought that nothing can operate against. Otherwise your word, unless it goes forth with power, speaking in a human way, would get tangled up in the false words. It must know itself. You must realize that, then you know it. You must know that your word is more than anything else. Otherwise your word will not amount to anything. The highest thought and the highest word are good through the omnipresence of God.

You are still dealing with the same law of cause and effect, and what the world needs today is to know and understand that law. And let each one apply to the limit of that law as much of the

Spirit as can be apprehended, and then the world will begin to get results. What you must begin at once to do is to protect yourself from man-made law concerning you. For instance, man has said that man is sick; now you must know, you must recognize that man has said it. You must recognize that the error is a thing over which you have absolute power, and you must know when you speak the word that your word has absolute power to destroy it. Thought is intelligence. You must know that what you say is destroying error. I do not want you to think you are antagonizing it or fighting, but in that calm assurance which comes to the individual who knows, you are destroying it. I should quite definitely speak the word that I knew would annul every law that seemed to me was the human cause of this thing. The time will come when we deal more and more with the absolute, but we have to approach that by degrees. If I have a case now that does not yield readily, I go over everything that we say causes that conditioning and I speak the word that destroys it. You will find your word has the amount of power, the amount of intelligence you put into it, and it has creative power according to the amount of absolute conviction and the impulse of love which is behind it. It has creative power according to that. Mind is that which is eternally self-conscious of itself, of its ability to do anything that it wants to, and whose one impulse is the impulse of love. That soul which can love the greatest will be the best healer, the one who can love the most universally, the one who can take into consciousness the broadest concept. All thought is impersonal, and we live in this Mind which immediately takes up whatever thought we think.

Suppose you have your business and you want to treat your business. You declare for the divine activity. Know first of all, you must realize this since it is the principle of everything, all is Mind. That must be very real in your consciousness; if you think something depends upon a condition, you are bound by that. First, you must know that all is Mind. Then you must know that the activity of Mind is thought. Next you must know that you are a thinker and that Mind takes up your thought and creates it. You must know that you are never dealing with a condition. Never look at the condition. If it is the healing of disease, never ask to see it. Never ask your patient how he or she is feeling, et cetera, and when your patient sits down for a treatment, if it is a disease, the first thing you have to do, in your consciousness, is to clear up all false thought they have been giving you. It is the same thing in your business; you must clear up all of the false consciousness which says that you are limited to thus and so, and when you get a clear concept that all is Mind governed through thought, that you are a thinker and you are a center of Mind, that thought makes your word more impersonal. Always, the more you can get away from personality, the better. That does not mean you should not care for people. We are living in Mind and there is nothing but Mind and its manifestation. Right then and there you begin to declare and make your declaration the eternal truth of Mind, then think, think impersonally, and you must feel you are stating the truth about the universal. That gives you a bigger concept and a bigger receptivity for a bigger power. The only reason I know for doing it is that you will get better results by doing it. You must feel like this. I am going to give a kind of a formula, not a formula, but a kind of a form around which you could weave your own words, for what I consider a very good way to give a treatment. Suppose we are taking a case of disease. First of all, we must recognize the absolute supremacy of Mind and Spirit. Then we must know there is no such a thing as people called corruptible, carnal; there is no such a thing as a physical person. I explain that in case some of you think there is no material person. If by physical you mean something

23

that is unspiritual, there is no such a thing. There is nothing but Mind or Spirit out of which a human can be made. We have been handling ourselves as if we are detached from Mind and Spirit, as if we were something entirely separate. There is no more intelligence in your finger than your mind puts in it. There is no physical human to operate in, upon, or through. Otherwise you will always find yourself fighting a condition. Realizing that, you must realize there is but one Mind and everything is the activity of that Mind and what you are doing is declaring the truth into that Mind and that Mind is going to execute the truth. Simply suppose I am A here and B is in New York City, or any distant city. A wants to give B a treatment. Some might tell B to sit down at a certain hour and get perfectly passive. That has nothing more to do with the meta-physical principle than my trying to hypnotize that chair. Here is Mind infinite, self-conscious. You are not trying to send a thought into the consciousness of your patient. That is a very, very danger-ous thing to do. Here is Mind, and we must know into it some-thing for the patient. That is all you could do anyway. The patient has asked for a treatment. Of course, the treatment has got to be-come effective in the patient's consciousness before it will heal. Here is the infinite principle that there is one Mind and we begin to know the truth about the patient and speak that truth into Mind. My responsibility begins when I begin to know the truth in myself, whether the patient ever gets it. You must know that it can heal; you must know that no thought of the patient, no suggestion against it, can operate against it. When you have known that, that is all there is to it.

I am going to treat B in New York City. That is all I have got to think about B, and I begin to state the truth. There is a power that is infinitely greater than we are. We will begin to get results. You are relieved of all responsibility. The sooner you get that, the quicker you will be able to work. So if you could work in just as impersonal a way as for yourself, you would obtain better results.

You have a business. Call your name into mind and begin to give your name a treatment, destroying in consciousness all false thought. If you get the right mentality, the business will be right. In order to help yourself the most effectively, you will have to learn to do it impersonally. There is nothing in my metaphysical work I make personal. I set the whole thing out into Mind. Suppose I get a letter from a person in San Francisco asking for a treatment. I begin immediately to declare the truth, and if a thought comes to me that this declaration of the truth is not sufficient, I begin again. How many people here have tried to give a treatment and felt that it was not sufficient? That is impersonal evil trying to make itself felt. As soon as that thought comes to you, turn and destroy it, erase it, get rid of it. Get it out of your consciousness and declare that this word is effective and it can produce, that it can, that it does, *it is*. Realize your word does it. If you do not learn to control your thought, thought will control you. What you have to do is with thought and not with people. If you are treating your own business, learn to get it right out in mind. If I want to give myself a treatment, say for a headache, I would give myself a treatment just the same as I would if you were manifesting that thought and you asked for a treatment. If I wanted to give myself a treatment for prosperity, I would take the same thing. I would begin to realize the truth about myself into Mind just the same as if I were treating somebody else. And now, the people who within their consciousness can get the clearest concept and expect most vividly the thing they are after will get it the quickest. But most of us are constantly declaring error. We are declaring I am sick, or weak, or unhappy, or Ernest Holmes has gone to hell. And here is Mind, that which eternally receives.

There are more people suffering from the race consciousness of condemnation. I have destroyed in my consciousness any belief in any punishment in hell. Then it was gone, then there was nothing there to make me sick. And when you destroy the obstruction that person sets up, the healing is done. *Health is.* You do not have to make it. *It is.* If you are sick, there is a negative thought there operating upon your body through your consciousness.

I must not only say, "I am not poor" because it sounds nice to say it, but there must be that within me spiritually that knows I am not; there must be a deep conviction within that knows all the truth of that which I say. Perhaps a million times I will have to do that over and over until I get over that false habit of thought. Whatever it is that hinders your progress is nothing but thought force working; and when you learn how to destroy it and get rid of it and know the truth, it will depart. Stop looking at the world as a conditioned thing governed by matter, matter, matter. Let matter alone. It is all right in itself.

We are getting ready to do some big things before the winter is over. I have seen such wonderful results, such marvelous results. I am surprised over them myself; in spite of the results I am surprised, and I can see such infinite possibilities just beyond. I want that every one of us shall prove this winter the absolute supremacy of our word. The thing to do now is to get your consciousness clear. I get so enthusiastic over this when I see the wonderful possibilities, when I see the people every day coming to me enjoying health, prosperity, and happiness. And when I know the infinite is just waiting to be acted upon. You are the actors. It is the binding thought of our own false consciousness that holds us. It seems as though I could not wait, and yet there is no use in talking to people who do not listen. A few do. And there is a possibility in this infinite storehouse of mind that God has made already for people to use and people ought to use it. We have got to learn the laws governing cause and effect—*law*. You have got to learn how to use it, and you have got to know how to use it, and then you have got to use it. I find those who get the best results are those who know what they are doing, constantly weeding out of their consciousness everything that hinders, destroying within them their false concept, a little here and a little there, and if they fall down, in not staying down but getting up and going on, over and over again. There is no practitioner who can do anything more for you than to help you. Your final emancipation will be written by your own hand or it will never be written at all; it will be thought out by your own mind. It will govern your own consciousness as it recognizes the supremacy of Mind, the infinite impulse of Spirit, and your own divine birthright to use it.

I have made a careful study since I have been investigating metaphysics. I have investigated it and proved it. I do not think we have a right to talk about anything we do not know about. I know that under the right systematic training of thought individuals can make themselves happy, prosperous, and well, and from that I believe there would be a state of consciousness that would do it at once. We have not arrived at that state of consciousness, and we have got to begin where we are. So that is what we must learn. Because we cannot speak some magic word and make something appear, because we cannot walk on water and pass through a wall, it cannot be said that it cannot be done.

This winter I would like to see 150 of us begin to systematically clear out of our consciousness everything that hinders it. Now, we can do that if we will work absolutely together as one, and take a certain line of consciousness each week and go after it scientifically, and come here and discuss it and find out what hinders it. I bet each person will look back and think it is an entirely different world. It takes time for us to grow the right kind of a consciousness. First, I had all of my own thought to overcome, my own observing of false condition. Then I also had to heal myself of what other people said about me. You start to do a new thing, and people will say it can't be done. They are making a law for you. Malpractice it is called in Christian Science.

You cannot in one bound, you cannot in one jump expect to find yourself renewed in body, soul, and mind and spirited into a new condition. But you do find, as I have, that a little here and little there is evident in your experience. Compare the consciousness today with what it was four or six months ago. As I compare the results, I find it is a new result I am getting. I find I am operating at a much higher law, and I find that my consciousness is even externalizing everything in the world. Four or six months ago it was a limited concept, it was a limited manifestation. There is a law of growth. We must learn to trust that law of growth, we must believe in it. If we will wait and know that, divine law and order will bring that thing upon us.

As sort of a preparation for our consciousness, those who intend to make this more or less of a permanent thing, let us begin this way: Follow one line of thought if you want to demonstrate. Your thought has not been clear on any one thing long enough to produce. Let us get our thought clear and picture it clear through.

As far as you are concerned, there is only causation; that is, Mind. This is your infinite principle of life. It is good, it wants to be, it can be all that you need. All that you will ever have comes from it, and all you ever have had came from it, and it comes flowing through your consciousness externalizing itself through the avenues of your thinking. We must learn to control our thought. And that is all we need to do.

To learn how to do this thing, we destroy false thought, we create the true and then know the true until that thing happens.

It is not only a privilege and a pleasure and a benefit to the individual because it gives them all that there is for all there is not, but I believe it is a solemn duty and obligation imposed upon every individual who believes this thing is true to prove it. I say it is a solemn obligation to you and to me to so prove this principle in our lives and so get such absolute, direct results that the world will sit up and know that the mental and spiritual principle is supreme. It is the only thing that will save the world from itself. The reason that Jesus never started a religion, or a center, or wrote a book, or started a church, or formed a government, all of which he could have done infinitely better than anybody that ever lived, is because he was the wisest man who ever lived; he never did these things because he left the complete unfoldment of understanding to take place after his exit from this world. He said, "The spirit of truth, when it comes to you, you will receive all things." Can you not see that it is when first this spirit is awakened within the individual that there is any inspiration, any power?

What we must learn to do is to scientifically dispose of everything that hinders this spirit from working. I know tonight that I have something with me which I cannot understand very much of, perhaps more than most people, perhaps less, but this I know: that I govern my life as I choose. I do that absolutely. And I do it through a law I have never seen. I know it works, for it never fails me. I know I have so much of that ability as I believe in, and I can see that Jesus, with his infinite understanding, could say, "Whatsoever ye believe, it will be done unto you." He understood the law of cause and effect. Right off, you know enough; begin to use it tonight. And right off begin to believe the word which you speak. That word which you speak is going to go forth and do the thing.

Know that it has the power, the intelligence, and know it is accomplished when you speak it. So it shall be to each one of us looking to the truth, believing in the absolute reality of the spiritual power of thought over everything else. For that reason, and for that reason alone, let us gather together with the determination to do it, it would convince 1,500. And so in this way, and it is the only way, the world will ever be saved. We may seem to be doing a small thing, but we are doing a thing which reaches throughout the universe. We are unified with that movement which will ultimately save the world.

Relief from
Responsibility

I want to begin next Monday evening the practice of the principles we have been attempting to teach these four or five Monday nights. I do not know how many there are who have been here every time, and I am interested to know, so will you kindly hold up your hands. That is good; I am glad to know so many have been in continuous attendance. The greatest trouble in teaching the truth is that you cannot get people present in one place long enough to teach it to them. They are like fleas, and then they wonder why nothing ever sticks to their feet. Nothing ever will.

Now, for the sake of those who really are in earnest and of course no other person in metaphysics could expect anything else to arrive, we are not dealing with some kind of a spiritual gymnastic stunt or a mental hocus-pocus, that you make a few passes with your mind or spirit and something happens. We are dealing with scientific facts insofar as they are known of the things that govern our life. We are dealing with Spirit and Mind, with Spirit and Mind and matter, the great trinity and unity, the great triune one. Spirit as causation, as impulse, as love, as intelligence. Mind as creative power, ever operative, ever creating, eternally making something; and matter, as the thing that it makes. You and I are dealing primarily simply with Spirit and Mind and the form in thought rather than the form in matter. We have learned in our experience that when we get the true form in thought and permeate it with the Spirit, we shall see the thing made flesh without any further effort on our part. We are dealing then with nature unseen and invisible, but we are more and more leaning on an invisible force operating upon an unseen plan. Now, it is not enough to teach this; it is not enough to hear it.

It is not enough to come here and learn that all is Mind. Every living individual has got to take that Mind and do something with it. The longer I study metaphysics, the plainer it becomes to me that it is just like everything else in life; there is very little that one soul can contribute to the welfare of another. Very little, indeed. There is very little that I can offer to you excepting to offer for your consideration that which I, as an individual, absolutely know to be true. I have yet to speak in public on anything that I have not proven. Two talks are all I have ever given in my life that I have not proven, and they were supposed to be theoretical and I announced them as such. It is not enough that I should know, and don't make the mistake that the ordinary person makes of thinking that it is enough. There is no treatment that I can give you that will make you prosperous. There is no treatment I can give you that will heal you; neither can any living soul.

There is a treatment that I can create or know for you which will set in motion for you a power of mind which is outside the objective knowing of both of us, and if you receive that it will heal you. The same with prosperity. There is too much in metaphysics, because there is as yet little understanding of this thinking that you can take a treatment and go out in the street and find money or be healed, when the cause is not cured that causes that disease. That is not the case.

The study of metaphysics is the study of the activity of Mind. It is the only activity there is in the universe. There is nothing that moves only when Mind moves it and there never was and there never will be any motion unless it is a motion of Mind. There was never a thing appeared on this planet but what there was a mental image behind the thing. So long as that mental image exists with the amount of vitality the almighty power has put in it the thing in objective life exists to destroy itself because the image is withdrawn. And what is the thing that moves everything? The study of metaphysics is the study of the Mind. We have everything that it is worth your time to know in psychology, but we do not teach it from the standpoint of limited psychology. We are studying Mind from the standpoint of its universal operation, and it is an entirely different thing. We are studying it from the standpoint that it is the only power that makes everything that is. We are thinking in Universal Mind and setting in operation therein for that individual a concept and it is received directly from the Universal Mind, and if it is received from It, It will heal them.

Now, it is the study of metaphysics, the study of Mind, the law of operation of thought, and we investigate a thing, we find we made a result, we say there must be a principle behind it. This is the way that advance has been made in all science of all times. They take something they know and from that they go out into the unknown always. And if you can do that, whether or not you can see the process and by using a certain combination of thought realize that thought, mind and spirit, using them as you see fit, is not only a power and a great power or some power or a wonderful power but that it is the only power. You get a certain result and it never fails, you have a right to say you have made a scientific discovery, and say there is a principle behind that, and provided you can prove that you have a right to draw the most far-reaching conclusions. And that is the way the principle of metaphysics has been discovered and taught, and today we know more about metaphysics than people did fifty years ago, or ten years ago, or five years ago. But the principle itself we do not know any more about than they did ten thousand years ago. We only know that we can use it. So the practice of metaphysics is the practice of a systematic system of thinking which arises from your consciousness. It is a systematic turning of all belief in limitation, in sickness, in death, in hell, in damnation, in evil, in everything that is unsatisfactory out of your thought and turning into your thinking everything that is just the opposite. Turn that which is negative into that which is beautiful, that which is loving, that which is harmonious.

I have no mind of my own to think with. In a certain sense I have, but there is Mind flowing through all. I want you to get this difference because it is all the difference between psychology and metaphysics. This is no criticism of psychology. Psychology is a preparation for metaphysics. All people who are teaching metaphysics, no matter what they call it, are teaching there is but one Mind and you and I are using it, and that Mind is all creative and all powerful and flows through our consciousness and makes what we think. There has never been a thought which you or I have projected through our consciousness but what this infinite mind created the thing for the thinker. I want you to see how important this is because next Monday night we are beginning the actual practice. I say mind is a self-conscious intelligence. Law is mind in action. Did you ever stop to think you cannot see any law? Behind it there is the unseen. That is what we call Mind. So all law is some activity of Mind doing something.

No living soul can contribute one iota of happiness or peace or health or happiness to your life, and no living soul can take one iota away only as you allow it to flow through your consciousness. And there is nobody here that knows that better than I.

If I am treating you, I am simply declaring into this Mind about you. That is what Jesus meant when he said, "It is done unto you." And you do not have to do it unto yourselves. With your limited thought, you would not know how to do it unto yourselves. I do not know what it is but we call it Mind, and that is as good a name as any for it. Its only instrument is thought and all law whether it is law that is today, this minute, causing your heart to beat, your blood to circulate and food to digest or whether it is the law holding this planet in its place. There is no time to Mind in action. Law is Mind in action. Did you ever stop to think you cannot see any law? Behind it there is the unseen. That is what we call Mind. So all law is some activity of Mind doing something.

Now, of course, Mind is intelligent. What we mean by intelligence is probably very limited, what we understand by intelligence. I say Mind is a self-conscious intelligence. It knows what it is doing and it is conscious that it is doing it. It knows how to think, how to reason, how to analyze. Of course, infinite Mind does not reason the way you and I do objectively. All of our reasoning is based on the supposition that somewhere there is a limit. Infinity knows there is no limit and could reason only from the supposition that behind the impulse is the Mind of God, I Am, and opposed to me there is nothing. And that is why God in the Bible is called I Am. This infinite I Am is the principle, is that which we announce as the principle through which we demonstrate. I do not doubt but what it is.

We speak forth into Mind and Mind takes our thought and does it unto us. No, that individual who can most implicitly believe that Mind is going to do it is the one who is going to get the biggest result. The person who sees Mind as law and through it an activity of Spirit, whose soul impulsion is God, I find that such people get remarkable results over the people who operate through a cold principle. Everybody has to, I cannot talk about my idea of God, that is my idea and my business and it could not be anybody else's, but there is an impersonal principle of Mind which does unto the thinker what he thinks, and the sooner you know it and learn to control your thought the sooner you will be able to heal your body and control your conditions, and until you do learn it your conditions control you. Now, bodies and conditions never operate or act; they are always operated and acted upon. Here lies the principle of demonstration. There are hundreds of thousands of people who are proving this.

Now, herein is the great relief from all responsibility, that Mind acts upon thought and you and I, I will say for the sake of clearness, we do not have to project into Universal Mind a definite thought or pattern or image or belief. Can't you see it is all the same thing? You may not get a definite knowledge of what you wanted, but you feel it; it is the same thing. Mind acts upon it and creates that thing, taking it as a pattern; Mind molds it out into what we call matter. Now, suppose you were healing Mary Smith in New York City. That is just what would happen. You would make all your statements of truth that form your realization of whatever you were going to do, but what you would be doing would be this: You would be directing Mind to act upon Mary Smith's body and it would heal it. It would operate through her consciousness. You would not be dealing with a physical body. For instance, here not so long ago I treated a certain individual for what is called a false growth, we will not name it. In this particular instance, I did not happen to see the person. There is no absence in thought. This is the way I thought, as near as I can remember:

I at first always try to realize within my consciousness that I am not dealing with matter. You see? I am not struggling to overcome a condition. Everything that appears in anybody's body is thought. There is not anything else to appear into form. I know if the thought is destroyed, the image of thought will leave the body. Here is this person and *Mind* and it has operated upon that person as a false belief. That person accepted it and may have been ignorant of it, but somewhere there is a picture in Mind or that itself would not be there. I am seeking to know the truth right where I am disregarding where they may be and as I succeed and they receive it will be done, and so I know I am not dealing with matter or a false growth at all; I am simply handling a false concept. And where am I handling it? I am handling it within myself, and when it is gone from my mind absolutely, remember this, as I know and that patient is receptive to law that patient will be healed, always. If the patient is not healed, then things have not been open; either the patient is not receptive or the practitioner has not realized it in Mind.

Realizing that I was not dealing with conditions, I was dealing with thought, I obliterate from my mind anything that says there is power in this false thought. I say my word has the power within itself to annul everything pertaining to this false thought. For instance, my word has the power of annulling the belief that people have got to be sick. It has the power to operate upon and annul every man-made law and it will leave nothing that says we can be sick, suffer, and die. It leaves nothing but pure Spirit substance. Do not think of the body itself in making your realization. I do not think I use many denials, but I use an affirmation. I would say my word annuls that so-called law. That covers all that is covered by a denial but at the same time erases the false concept. People sometimes wonder if they are good enough to heal. Of course you are, but you will not always have the same degree of consciousness. You can be just right. You do not have to be abnormal or unnatural. Be an impulsive sort of a person just like everybody else.

Every living soul that lives is dealing with universal law and they cannot help it. If God knew sin, God would be a sinner. You and I must know with our thoughts. All disease is the result of wrong thinking somewhere. There is no such thing as a sinner unless it is you and me. It all comes from false thought, and you and I must know that our word is the power to annul that. Since everything is Mind in a neutral state, an impersonal, receptive, and creative state whatever is thought into Mind, Mind is going to do. If you have thought all of your life that you were so and so and could be sick, that has got to be annulled in Mind about you. And that is the difference between psychological healing, which suggests to the mentality of the patient that things are all right, and as long as that hypnotic state holds over them they are well but there is almost invariably a reaction. Nine out of every ten people who are healed by psychological methods have a relapse. There is very seldom a relapse in metaphysical healing. Because it is the belief in Mind about them.

I can only just touch on the steps. I have studied and thought this for seven or eight years and worked it out, and have found out more by practice than any other way and more by thinking and applying it. Whatever you will get out of this you will get out of yourself. After hearing about it, you have got to take these things and think them out for yourself. If they are not true, it is the biggest fake in the world. Many people think they are wonderful thinkers, and they are not thinking at all. To think is to think right

38

straight through to the bottom until there is nothing left to think about, to find out about that particular thing. If anything comes up in your experience and you want to dissolve it, there is a mental reason behind it. Now, for the ordinary individual in a sort of weak-kneed way, there is too much hanging on somebody else's neck. Either hang on your own neck or hang by the neck. There is a mystery to nothing except the mystery of life, and nobody knows anything about that. If anything comes up in our lives, we want to know how to get rid of it, and get right and if I can get right in 100 years on this planet I do not care where I came from and where I am going. I want to be 100 percent efficient today and be a normal human being active and living. One hundred percent efficient to the human race. And that is all we need. And if something comes up in your life that ought not to be, or in mine, I must not necessarily find out the reason and yet I must cover the reason with the truth. For instance, you take a person who is always unhappy. Now, there is something wrong in that life. Is it a feeling of loneliness? It must be healed. That thing must not only be changed but, if that person is suffering because of a lack of friends, it must be faced scientifically, working it out, attracting friendship. That Mind that is me is in you and when I know within my mind that which is truth it will draw unto me whatever I want or whoever I want, not that I operate on them, I know nothing about them. It is because it is the one Mind flowing through all and unifying everything that is alike through the great law of attraction. Like attracts like always.

Poverty is an abnormal condition. Poverty is the result of inefficiency. Poverty is not the result of the lack of opportunity. Not in yourself, not anywhere. Poverty is the result of inefficiency, or ignorance. And if you and I can learn to deal with the only Mind there is, we will no longer be poor. We can attract to ourselves people and things which will obliterate that poverty. It will be a law of gravity, no other thing but principle. When you set in motion a power of mind, don't you be surprised what happens; don't be surprised if something comes from the most unheard-of source ever dreamed of. So it was with an unusually big thing that someone wanted some help on. It involved a very large expenditure on somebody's part, and when these people brought it to me there had been no activity for several years, but it was a perfectly legitimate proposition, and I said let's try it. I said, If we can believe that we are dealing with a power that is infinite that power will direct the way, and so I treated it every day. After a little while there were inquiries for the first time in years and by and by different parties and different things came into it, and then in a few more weeks the thing was done. That was the direct answer to a metaphysician's way of praying.

I had an argument in a legal way over that. A man said this was not prayer, and I said it was prayer because it was our way of invoking Divine Intelligence to bless us. It is our way of praying. We believe that when we speak, that word is the very presence and power and activity of as much of God as we believe in while we speak, and to prove it, most remarkable things happen. I am telling you all these things in sort of a jumble.

Everybody has got to heal themselves; there is no other way. I can tell you these things, but you have to make the application. These are pointers. Another thing, be absolutely impersonal about your work. Suppose I wanted to treat myself for something. I call my own name right out in Mind and treat it just the same as if it were somebody I never heard of before, just as disinterestedly as I can, so that the consciousness of fear will not crowd.

I find this, and it is the experience of all metaphysicians and the more you can work that way the better results you can get. You get a greater consciousness than you do when you bear in your consciousness the limitation of your limitations and your fears. Do not limit your affirmations about God. Link God up with yourself, for we see there is one life, perfect, that is God. I have got to see this life is in me now. That is what made Jesus the Christ; he said, "My Father and I are one." Be absolutely impersonal.

Another thing: Do not treat yourself too much. If you want to, treat yourself as many as three times a day for about ten or fifteen minutes, three times a day to realize the truth. Of course, you must have this if you expect to get results. If you cannot do it, then it is perhaps a good practice to begin with to first of all get absolutely at one with yourself. No disgruntled, unhappy sort of a person can do much in metaphysics. That would be the first thing to begin with, so you can get a sense of peace and satisfaction, calm and serenity. There must be a center there. You are dealing with a power that is absolute. It is a conception that is limitless. It learns things out of itself. God makes things from what you think. Everything comes into visibility from the invisible.

Know it no longer has any power over you, that thing which denies the right of mind, then affirm the truth until you realize the thing that is. More and more you will realize that you are dealing with things. Faith is a mental attitude which actually takes hold of the substance which exists and brings it right before the eyes of the person as an evidence that the thing did exist. The Bible says, "The things which are seen are not made of the things which do appear." Now then, that is true of all life and you must know it. You must know this and it is a most important part of your treatment, that we are going forth into mind. We are not a projection of God; we are not a manifestation forth from God; we are not a reflection of an image forth from God. We are at the center of God consciousness. And it could not be otherwise. There is nothing but what we call God to make you out of. Whatever there is of you is something or some part of God because there was nothing else to make you out of. So know that you are a center of God consciousness and that is why your word is infinite. Speak it forth believing and never doubt it. You know, you just believe, and then you speak forth this word knowing that it annuls everything which seems to oppose it. It annuls that so-called law of matter. Know that it is the law of harmony and adjustment. It is the law of justice, for that is what you need. It is the law of balance. It is the law of increase. It is the law of plenty. It is the law of activity, if there is no activity. It is the law of attraction, if you need something. It is all that there is, and you realize that that word becomes; it goes forth upon this power implicitly.

You will treat until you just feel sure within yourself that that is true. Then you will go about your business in a normal sort of way, being very careful and watching how you think. Feel that you have planted in the soil of Mind the seed of definite thought. The law of growth will operate upon it. Declare that it is eternal, that it can fulfill, that it will work and work until it perfectly fulfills itself.

So in our practice during the coming weeks we are going to come right along and work out definite problems. I want you to come next Monday night with definite problems. Take as many things as you can think of clearly. But whatever you do, be definite; I know of no other way to demonstrate unless you are definite. There is no other way. I see in this universe nothing but evidence of definiteness, and I am compelled to believe that intelligence is definite. Every planet appears definitely in a place and is definitely controlled, and if we are going to deal with intelligence, we have got to deal with it in a definite manner. Nothing is left to chance in this universe. Everything is working by the perfect law of cause and effect. If an individual tells you that she has had a great revelation from God, tell her to prove it through cause and effect; be absolutely definite. Know what you want. When Jesus turned the water into wine, they had asked for wine. He did not turn it into buttermilk.

We will take these things up, each one realizing that there is a Universal One which manifests itself into a multiplicity of ideas and also that it can manifest as many things for us as we can conceive. So, taking these definite things, let us see that it will definitely work. We will take certain forms. You can work spontaneously for one week and then we shall take definite forms. So we shall each learn what the metaphysical principle is by demonstrating it. It is the only way. Let us be something definite and do something and do it well. We will learn by doing and not by reading, or hearing, but by doing.

Demonstrating from an
Invisible Principle

The metaphysical principle can be demonstrated; there is not any question about that. It is not any good unless it can be. It can. You can draw from an invisible principle which receives your thought and acts upon it just what you believe you will get. Now, there is not any question about that. I want to say again that what that principle is further than that it must be mind, of its real nature I am profoundly ignorant and so is everybody else, and it is useless to make any claims that we cannot substantiate. There is not any living soul knows what God is. We say God is the life essence of all that there is. That is true, but it can be said of electricity that no living soul knows what electricity is, but electricity *is;* we may as well use it.

Mind *is* and we may as well use that. It is productive of wonderful results when we contact it in the right way. There is no longer any question but what we are surrounded by something and we call it mind which receives every impress of our thought and which acts upon every impress of our thought and tends to bring it out into outer manifestation; so that if you and I want to entertain a mental concept long enough, it would be created for us. There is no question about that.

You and I do constantly entertain mental concepts; indeed, we cannot help it. We are thinking beings and we cannot help thinking. It depends then upon what we think what we shall become, and the sooner individuals who are seeking to operate this principle will realize that it depends only upon what they think, and depends upon nothing else, and the sooner they learn to depend upon nothing else, the sooner they will demonstrate that principle. To any thinking person there must come a time when there is a realization that everything which is seen comes from that which is not seen; that, since that which is not seen is the cause of everything, it is also the effect of everything—that is, it is the cause behind it, that it is the effect in manifestation and that the whole process of creation takes place on an invisible plane, absolutely. We are learning that this creative process is the result of some activity of thought in Mind, whether it is God's thought or your thought or my thought. When we think, our thought, we will say goes forth, is immediately surrounded by this Mind that immediately begins to act upon it, just like the creative power in the soil acts upon the seed. When I first realized this it took me a long time to think it out, or study it out. You learn more by thinking than you will in any other way, and I came to the conclusion that it must be this way, that it could not be any other; then it took me several years to get where I could use it. I had to go by something that I believed but was not sure of. I realized this, and there is a point to consider, that since all is Mind and when you and I think that Mind creates it, it can only create what we think, no more and no less.

So long as we entertain a negative attitude toward any proposition we are destroying any possibility of that thing happening.

For instance, suppose I was sick and wanted to heal myself, so long as I hold thoughts of sickness within my mind I could not heal myself. It is not easy to think you are well when you think you are sick. It is not easy, if you are in business and everything seems to be going wrong, to mentally rise above that which appears on the outside, and so I used to reason this out in this way. I will plant a seed in the garden. Now, I do not see any life in the seed, I do not see any creative power in the soil; all that I know is this—the seed is and the soil is and we have always known if we put a seed in the ground we would get a plant and that proves there is a law of growth, a law which is creative, which is productive, a law which is receptive, a law which is eternal. It will take any kind of a seed, it does not care who puts it in the ground, it is impersonal, anybody can plant a garden and if they comply with the conditions of soil and water it will grow. What is true of one plant is true of all. And what is true on the outside, since it is the external manifestation of the concept held in the Spirit, must be like that which made it; like produces like. We draw nothing from nothing, something has to come from something, and wherever you find anything in the physical universe you find something that upholds it and that is universal and omnipresent and intelligent. And so I used to think about myself, that same thing happens. I have no responsibility except to create the right kind of a mental receptivity. That is the truth. Thus we, who are seeking to demonstrate, we know that all we have got to do is to realize the truth, that is, use the mind in a positive formative way and the Mind, or the power which creates everything and projects it, will do the rest for us. Until we come to the point where we see that this is all we have to do, it is all thought; no matter how hard we struggle, we could not do anything else. All we have to do is to take up the attitude of the expectant receiver, realizing we are scientifically using the law.

A couple of months ago I was seeking to make a demonstration which in a certain way was quite important for myself, a thing which seemed quite a necessary thing to have. And I struggled quite a bit, a thing I do not often do. (Learn never to put anybody on a pedestal. If you put them up high enough you will invariably see their feet are made of clay.) I did struggle considerably with my thought, trying to work it out myself, then I said, I am all wrong here. If there is a power working this out for me, I have to prove my absolute reliance upon it, I have to let it alone. And so I went about and thought no more about it and today in the most unaccountable way that thing was made possible. Something that would never have entered my consciousness in a thousand years, and it shows that if we dare, and learn to place implicit trust, there is something that honors that faith which we give it.

The subjective side of an individual's thought does not mean another mind. It means the accumulation of race belief which we accept operating through us. The thought forms which we have created and with which we have surrounded ourselves, our mental beliefs underneath, the result of our objective thinking and receiving through race suggestions, is termed subjective consciousness; it is that power of attraction or repulsion which the individual mentally sets up within. That is the subjective side of your mind. It is not another mind. It is your own mind operating; that is all. Your life and mine depend upon the subjective side of our thought. Who we are, as well as what we have in health, or wealth, or peace of mind will be the result of the accumulation of our thinking, always. It could not be anything else. Now, we are going a step farther and not only saying in peace of mind and character, but in individual health and physical environment, and I know it is true.

Relieve yourselves of all responsibility of making anything. You could not make anything if you tried to. The united intelligence of the human race from time immemorial summed up into one moment could not create one petal of one rose, because it does not know enough to do it, and it is good that it does not. But it can have created for it as many roses as it sees fit through using the creative principle which is, and it need not take the responsibility of that creative power at all. So when we come to our responsibility, it rests solely in providing the right atmosphere and nothing else. I am giving you a system of thought, and if you want to make a demonstration you can work it out. I would not do it for you if I could. I would be depriving you of a divine right. From the metaphysical standpoint, I say get your arms away from clinging on other people. Dare to be yourself. Where did you think anybody ever got so much that you could not know? Then and there you are foreswearing yourself. I am just as intelligent as anybody who ever lived. You have got to have a kind of a decent idea of yourself in metaphysics. Did you ever see a person succeed in business who thought it would fail? You never did and you never will. People who succeed in life are the people who know that they will. And that free knowing is creation in the mind of the Universal. You must do this all for yourself and know this for yourself. It is working for me every day I live.

There is One, and not two. Never forget that. Anywhere in the universe, just One. That one life is the substance of everything. It is one in unity but multiple in manifestation. It is one substance from which an infinite variety of different things come but every one of those things is made out of the one thing. Now, that one life and intelligence and creative power operates through me, that is the next thing. It would not be of any good to us if there was one infinite life unless that life was in some way connected up with me. Many people make a mistake in thinking it is enough to claim that God is all. We must realize there is one Power, one God, one

All, one Life, and that life is in me now. I am a manifestation of that One.

Now you have a working principle. You can think of yourself as a sort of a center in this Divine Living Intelligence through which It operates. Begin to think of your consciousness as an activity of mind through which It flows. Begin to think of your word as the word of power going into it which shall create. That brings you to the One. This mind makes everything. The spirit, or God, makes everything by thinking, or speaking, and then the thing appears in the visible, and since that life is in you, in your word, you do the same thing. You can look at your hand every day and declare that there is a wart right there and it will come. Your word will manifest. You can look at it every day for a while longer and declare that it is gone and it will go, provided you arrive at a consciousness that knows.

This Infinite One cannot know anything outside of Itself. Anything that would say "I am not a part of It" It would not recognize at all because that would be a contradiction of Its divine nature. So, when you say, I am poor, I am sick, or weak, or I am not one with the creative power, you are using that creative power to keep yourself away from the Infinite, and just as soon as you declare you are one with God, there is a rushing out to meet you— just as the father rushed out to meet the prodigal son. Jesus said, "The spirit seeketh." So long as your mind is in the term of conditions you cannot overcome.

Here is the way to do it. You are not dealing with conditions. Overcome it. To think of disease creates it. You are dealing only with thought, thought, nothing else, thought and Spirit. Spirit is the thing that thinks in you and so you are dealing only with the activity of Spirit which is thought, and you must believe that that thought is law. For instance, I want you to take this and practice it.

Suppose you are in business, remember this law will work anywhere for anything; it will kill you just as quick as it will save you. Do not forget that. It could not be law if it would not work that way. If you use it to do that which is not in harmony with the fundamental principles of good, sooner or later you will be very sorry, but that will not be anybody's business but your own. If a person takes this and uses it in a wrong way, that is up to them. But I do not think people want to use it in a wrong way. I think if there is anything known about the law and how it works, it should be their life endeavor to tell as many people about it as they can. You sit then in that business and you want to demonstrate activity; in other words, you want more customers. You want many people coming and going, buying and selling. You can demonstrate that in a very easy way, provided you will believe. First of all, there is one power, and it is in you. Then, for the sake of clear thinking, you state it definitely, say it right out. Now, this word which is spoken is the law about this thing about which I am speaking. Realize that that law is to be a universal thing. Your word is to go to the universal power which recognizes it. This word is the law unto this case.

There is something in the race suggestion which says that all is matter. You have got to destroy that about your thought. That is held in the race consciousness over every individual and binds them hand and foot until they are emancipated. You have got to destroy that race consciousness. Then you state definitely, *This word which I speak destroys every man-made belief, it destroys the thought of nonactivity, it annuls the thought of lack, it destroys the thought that there is not plenty.* If race suggestions happen to be the means which hold you, and no doubt they will until you destroy them, then you have got to destroy them. If the race suggestion is that nobody wants to buy this kind of a thing, you have got to destroy that by declaring absolute activity is here. When you make your declaration like that, there is a power upon which you can absolutely and unconditionally rely. It is not enough to say God is good and all is lovely. I believe that is a beautiful thing to say and I am quite sure it is the truth, but it will never save you. God is good, but you are your own savior. It could not be otherwise. Jesus could not save. God cannot save. Why? Because every living soul is an individual and we are let alone to work out our own destiny. Let us each then turn to the God who is good and immediately we are reinforced by an infinite power working in and through our divine individuality. So don't hesitate to destroy every thought that is held in the race consciousness. Then you declare there is but one power that overcomes and that is the one and it is right here now, and the impulse of that word which you speak goes out and it establishes here and now the law of divine harmony and activity. It will work. I have proved it a thousand times for a thousand different people, and I have yet to see it fail if the conditions are complied with.

The next condition then is that you have got to provide within your own consciousness some kind of a unity with the thing you want; that only stands to reason. The person who is not used to doing big things in life will not immediately begin to do them. That person's consciousness has got to expand, has got to grow, to apprehend more and more ability to grasp things, and so there is a law of growth in the individual. The law springs spontaneously from the Spirit, but the concept has to grow from the individual. We have got to provide a mental equivalent for everything we want. If I want to create activity, I must realize in my life what great activity means. For instance, a man who has all his life sold peanuts for five cents a gob and taken in three or four dollars a day and paid out two or three dollars won't know very much about handling big propositions and doing business on a big scale. That man has got to begin right where he is, and everybody has got to begin right where they are. Do not be surprised if someone did not come along in two or three weeks and give you a million dollars. But be satisfied if within your own consciousness you can see a mental unfoldment, a greater reaching out and taking in more and more, and when you feel your vision is enlarging, as it enlarges just reach right out and take hold of everything. For instance, this is a habit I have in my life: It may be right or it may be wrong; it does not matter. I constantly unify myself with the activity of the human race. It is not enough that I sit here and say, I hope a half a dozen people come to my class, but that I get such a large grasp of things that the whole world will come in trying to manifest them, the one living activity, absolute and eternal. The trouble with the human race and the individual seeking to demonstrate is this: They are so confounded personal, so selfish, so egotistical they cannot see, they cannot get a grasp of the big things because their sense is limited to personal things, me and my wife, my son John and his wife; biscuits for four of us, thank God there are no more of us. We have got to get over that little suggestion; it is not enough. To become alive and build the greatest lives we must become something more, something worthwhile. There is not a day in my life that goes by that I do not take the time to unify myself in my consciousness with big things, to think I am one with all activities, all industries, all commerce, et cetera, et cetera, and just feel that thought reaching out and encompassing the largest fields of activity of the world. Then you are one with the infinite stars in the heavens, and that is to see things. It is that in our mental attitude that decides what we are to become and nothing else. If you could feel your mental concept of your business touch the universal, you would only have to speak the word and it would come to you in a ceaseless stream. At first you will have to do this mechanically. I have in mind one woman who said, "That is true and it is true for me." She has made more financial demonstrations and secured more success and got more absolute results than anybody I have had in my class in a year's time, and she has done it in three months. She said, "That is it, that is just what I am looking for." I believe I am just fool enough to do it. And I have never seen such remarkable results in so short a time. It was pretty hard to convince myself that the thing was true at all. But there was something in me that knew it had to be true. I could see the results could not be if it were not true. But the old race suggestion would come up. I fought it. We ought not to have to fight. We ought not to have physical war, but we have got it and that is why we are fighting. There is nothing to concentrate on; the very act of trying to concentrate will destroy the very possibility of demonstrating. But calmly and persistently, even though it be mechanically, you speak the word and there is a certain amount of power. And gradually you will be able to feel the form of the word is the letter of the law with the flesh and makes it become the real thing. But at first, if you cannot do it any other way, just do it mechanically. Say it over and over again, and put as much of the spirit into the word as you can get to put into it. Convince yourself over and over again. Suppose you wanted to attract to you some opportunity, some definite thing. You do the same thing, let it be known in mind what you want and then within yourself provide a perfect embodiment of the expression which you want. Become that thing. Jesus said, "That I have and I shall become it." Feel yourself to be that thing, feel yourself surrounded by all of the conditions that that environment embodies and then speak right forth knowing that word is law, knowing that is the way it is.

And another thing: More and more realize that intelligence

knows. You are not dealing with a blind force; you are dealing with something that knows, something which is—intelligence is eternally creative and not the intelligence of the human race.

You have got to practice these things. Take a few moments each day in silence and recognition of Infinite life; Affirm one, It is in me now; two, I can use it, my word goes forth into mind; three, It takes my word and creates it; four, I see in my life the thing which it has created.

Taking that as a proposition, you can handle as many things as you want to—as many as you can carry in mind.

Literally speaking, you and I are in an infinite mind which creates for us. Now, then, you can take thought and speak it forth with absolute conviction.

The length of time you must treat: You might have to treat an hour before you believe what you state. *Think about it until you absolutely think that is the truth.*

Do it two or three times a day, until there is a perfect calm confidence, knowing that it is done.

A lady who has really gotten a rather remarkable consciousness has made a very wonderful demonstration of the power of the word a short time ago on a fig tree. The figs would grow about so far and would not grow any more. She spoke the power of the spirit and said, "I know it is still in these figs and there is some wrong thought which hinders them from bursting through." It seems some neighbors had said that the figs on that tree would only grow about so big and then fall off. "That," she said, "is what hinders them. Something was wrong but I do not know what it was, and I am going to treat that tree until I know that which is perfect about it." She thought of all of the things that were said in the Bible that Jesus had done about material things. She worked until she knew that tree was full of perfect figs. She did not go out to see until the next morning, and she found the figs had doubled in size. I do not know as it is wise to tell these things in public because the public is awfully unbelieving. Do you know that fig tree was nothing but a mental concept and it is created perfect and that mind can and does control even the plants? Do you know how Luther Burbank gets results? He talks to his plants. He is a metaphysician, and that is the way he gets them to grow. There is a law that the florist will find the flower before the seed. That has got to be. Nothing comes from nothing; only something has to come from something. Don't you know that those people have the best success with plants who love them. Be that as it may.

This thing we are to work upon. That power is in you, but you have got to bring it forth. It is latent in every living soul, but you have got to bring it out.

The *following is an example of a treatment which creates a demonstration:*
Realize you have nothing to make, you have nothing to make it out of. Let us realize there is but one Infinite Life from which all things come. Look beyond all manifestation and see the One Power, Essence of All That Is, beside which there is nothing else. That life is in me now; *That Life is in me now.*

Now, my word is to go forth; everybody must think it through for themselves as I am thinking it through for myself. Your word is just as much as mine; my word goes forth into this power and it shall be done unto me absolutely as I believe.

I believe that the Spirit or Intelligence hears this word and receives it and acts upon it.

There is nothing in me, no doubt or fear, that can hinder it. That thing which calls itself doubt or limitation and fear is not any part of me. It is not me. This word which I speak destroys every false concept, every man-made law, every race suggestion of limitation, and knows itself to be power, and perfect, and eternal, and complete, and omnipotent. *It is the law which cannot be broken.*

That word which is within me and around me, the divine activity of the Spirit which is eternal, drawing to me, presenting me with every good and perfect thing, surrounding me with its own limitless activity and power, operating within me as the power and center of infinite attraction. The great impulse of this Spirit is love and expression, to express life. Therefore, this word goes forth with an irresistible power; nothing can stand against it. It returns unto me fulfilled in my life as activity, as supply, and if I desire some special activity I will say that this word, this great Mind which knows every living soul, knows that particular person that has need of that; I have and will draw them to me, and I need never know until they come.

Mind knows all, is in all, flows through all, and within and without all and encompasses all. And so that person who comes shall be benefited even as I shall be benefited.

Now I consciously unify myself with all of the activities of power and of right on earth. I am one with all the wealth of the earth and the air and the sea and the land, and everything that is in the universe is mine to use.

And behind it all, and in and through and in and around it all, permeating myself and the thought and the law, is the living spirit and presence of that Being whom we call God Almighty, the One and Only Presence, Divine and Eternal Power, the Infinite Companion.

Thou God Eternal, Thou has heard my prayer and I am blessed.

This word, then, which I speak is absolute, complete, changeless, eternal truth, forever.

Just realize it. Let it go and realize that it is taken up by the power which knows. That is all there is to making a demonstration. You must believe it as the great reality of your life.

It is the law of life that you should give as you receive. It is not a suggestion for a large collection, because the collections have been unusually large during this season of talks, but we can always give as we hope to receive. We have always found in our word that classes are very liberal, and we get what we give.

People who expect to demonstrate this principle must be very constant, very determined, very positive, very sure, and faithful with themselves, patient with themselves, long-suffering with themselves. You will rise and you will fall, you will get discouraged, you will become encouraged, but always you will be progressing, always, and so you must simply stick to it and the day will come when you will no longer say, "I hope, I desire, I pray," but you will say, "I know." You can hasten that day by doing away with all argument now and simply accepting it. You can hasten your progress. The weary steps can be done away with if we can accept it at once. Had I been able to begin the first day where I did begin, the truth would have operated just as quickly.

Bring to mind a definite problem and treat on that definite problem until you get the solution. Take two dozen different things if you can keep them in mind.

Don't come and think you go through some spiritual trick and it is done. It will be done when your consciousness corresponds with the thing you desire.

Attracting the
Great Big Things

In metaphysics, as in everything else, if we want to accomplish results, we have got to do something with our principle. It is not enough to say all is Spirit and all is Mind. That won't heal you. It is not enough to say God is good. That will never do it. God is good; that might be a part of it. Everything in the universe is good, but if we are actually to change our conditions and heal our bodies, we have to take the principle of life and scientifically apply it. It is not enough for you and me to sit down and say electricity is and electricity is wonderful and it is illuminating. Unless we take the principle of electricity and apply it for a definite purpose, it will not illuminate anything. The reason more people do not succeed in metaphysics in the way of demonstrating is that they do not realize that Mind has to be applied. They think they can sit down and say God is good and God is all and that will do it. Now, it won't do it, and the people who do not do more than that do not get results. The people who get results realize the mental principle, realize they get results in the universe through mental law and that they govern in their own life through mental law and they begin to use that mental law of causation, creative power, and allow it to flow through them. They begin definitely to use it as a great law of attraction setting up within their own consciousness a center for a definite purpose and realizing that toward that center there will gravitate the thing they desire; realizing there is a power behind it which is intelligent, which makes it operate, which relieves them of personal responsibility so that all the individual has to do is to know within. And that person who can know the most definitely and the most clearly and at the same time with the greatest sense of ease and peace, devoid of all fear, being absolutely sure, that is the person who will make the best demonstration.

There are but a few points you must always remember: Since all is Mind and the only activity of Mind is thought, and the only thing you get out of Mind is what you first think into it, what you think is of the greatest importance. How you think it, the bigness with which you think it: If you could only conceive a very small thing, that is all you would physically get. Here we realize that we are not dealing with anything that is physical. There is no physical explanation for anything on earth or anything else and there never will be. All manifestation is backed up by a definite idea. Every idea is a thought in your life and mind and everything that happens to us is backed up by some mental attitude.

We have on the one hand all Mind, or the substance which forms itself around our thought; on the other hand, we have the thought around which it forms. And here is something you must never forget: that Life can only operate for us by flowing through us, never in any other way.

You will never demonstrate until behind your mental attitude is the belief that you have received before you have received that thing which is sought. And if you will study the life of any successful businesspeople, they are doing the same thing uncon-

sciously. All we are doing is learning to take the same thing and
systematically apply it for definite purposes, and it operates. The
reason why so few people succeed, and yet I am surprised at the
large number who do succeed and get some result, but the reason
why more people do not is that in the first place they are not able
to separate things and effects and realize they have nothing to do
with them. As an effect, as a thing, as an objectified object, neither
your body nor conditions act; they are both acted upon. They of
themselves cannot act. They are devoid of intelligence and are always acted upon by your mentality. So, it is not easy, it is just as
hard for me as for anybody (probably easier if one has more practice), it is not easy to get rid of the objective thing. It is not at all
easy to get rid of it, but you have to get rid of it.

About two weeks ago I received a letter from Nova Scotia, a
man asked me to treat him. I never heard of him and I don't know
how he heard of me. I was very busy and I asked my mother to
treat him, for I knew she could treat him just as well as I could.
After she had given the treatment she said, "That person was
healed, whoever he was, I got such a clear consciousness of life, I
know he must have been healed." Today I got another letter, he
thought I had treated him (that's pretty bad for me to tell a thing
like that); I got another letter from the same town from another
person, saying it was an instantaneous healing, and this one wanted
somebody else there to be treated. The thing of it was this, that
often you can do better if you do not see the thing you are working for. You get a clearer consciousness and since all is Mind and
since Mind is omnipresent and all-knowing, when we make the
perfect realization in Mind, never forget that, what you have to do
is to make the perfect realization in Mind, not in the mind of the
patient, not in your mind, but in Mind, the only mind there is, and
so far as you are concerned that Mind flows through you and there-

fore you get the realization in your consciousness and, since Mind is one, it is made in Mind. And upon your ability to know perfect life, that is what gives you your ability to heal. I do get disgusted when people use this thing and think of it simply as a sentiment. It is more. It is a scientific fact; *Mind is.* But we have got to contact it in the order that it works; we have got to use it ourselves, the law of cause and effect. We have got to use it just the way it is; we cannot change it, but we can use it. It is an eternal force. I do not know any more about it than you do, and nobody else on earth knows. When we use it in a certain way, we get results. So you can know perfect law, know that your word destroys everything that is imperfect, breaks down every man-made law, every material law, and know that your word is the law unto this case.

This is for demonstration. Suppose you sit down in front of a patient who had tuberculosis. Now, that patient is dying because something is operating upon his body. We know that since all causation is Mind, whatever is operating on that individual's body is some activity of Mind, or thought, we call it race consciousness. The whole race consciousness is that tuberculosis kills people, but it is all mental. That chair has not got tuberculosis, and that body has no more mind than the chair; it is made out of the same kind of stuff. It is acted upon by some thought which probably did not start spontaneously in his own consciousness, that individual probably had not wanted to become sick, but he had become receptive to the race consciousness and had taken in a lot of negative thought. If you sit down beside this patient and say, "This poor fellow has tuberculosis and that is pretty bad and I am going to see what I can do for him. Maybe I can do as well as anybody else, but it looks to me like kind of a hopeless thing, but I will do the best I can for him," you will never be able to heal him. So long as you are treating that man's body as a physical body, you cannot heal him metaphysically. That is one of the great errors in metaphysics. That man's body is nothing but an effect; it is an outpicturing of his mind and is just as fluent and plastic as water when you pour it from one pitcher to another. Forget the body altogether. You can work only in Mind because that is causation.

Here is another mistake; here is a psychological mistake, or a mistake of psychology. I cannot plaster my thought into his. That would mean you had a mind and he had a mind. That is not the truth because there is nothing but Mind and you are both in it, and in this race consciousness there is thought operating against this Mind and that is where we have got to destroy it. Do you understand? Then, what are you going to do? First, you must realize that you are a mental being, or spiritual; you are perfect; and your word is perfect—it is absolute. This is not taking anything away from God. God is still God, and God is still All. But you are recognizing that God has given you power also as God has. You have got to know absolutely that your word is the law unto this case; it is. If it was not, you could not heal anything. So then, quite definitely I would state to begin with, and often I have to do it now, I declare often, "My word is the law unto this case, absolutely." And it is not enough just to declare that word with a sort of empty meaning; that must be backed up by the consciousness that recognizes what you mean. You must feel that beyond your word there is an infinite power, an intelligence that is causation; it is right out into it. That is making your unity with the Infinite. Then, you know your word destroys every man-made law that anybody has made about this person that says the man is poor and sick and miserable and has to die of tuberculosis. Your word must have that power itself of casting out. Let nature alone; it is perfect always.

Then your word has destroyed that false thought and establishes the divine law of harmony, and you declare this man to be perfect and you realize perfect life for him. And there is something, I do not know what it is, does it. It is senseless for anybody to get up and tell about what God is. I think when people begin to talk like that it is a sign of weakness. We just know there is something that does it. And it will do it and correspond absolutely to our mentality when we do it. We know that something behind it must be infinite and we seemingly are finite. I suppose in reality whatever our life is, is some part of the great life; it must be since we are in it. But this is quite sure, that that individual who gets the biggest concept of what we call life is the one who gets the biggest flow into his or her word and so it has the biggest power. We are too little, too picayunish, too personal, too full of those nasty little things we think of ourselves and others. We have got to accept things in a big, big way. My idea of health is that *health is*. It is complete; it is being. I do not think of health as having any degrees as good, better, best. You cannot compare that which is perfect, and anything that denies it is imperfect. And so we should take as our standpoint the highest possible thought we can have.

Somebody has well said, "God is our highest conception." Always has been since time immemorial. As our concept of life has enlarged, our concept of God has enlarged more and more until now we reach out and say it is universal and omnipotent. And since that is the highest concept we have come to know, it is the best we have. Sometime we may have a better one.

As long as you and I are too personal, suppose I sit down in front of that person and say, "I've got to heal him. It is a big job." I could not do a thing. My consciousness has got to realize that Mind is universal, that it knows everything, that it is all-powerful at all times. The time will come when one's consciousness will be so strong that they will heal as they pass along, that one can heal a thousand people at once. There is such a state of consciousness.

About half the time when I give a treatment I spend two or three minutes giving a treatment. Just as soon as you get that bigness of thought and you know it, it is a treatment, and you could not do anything else. You cannot make anything happen. People have tried to make things happen, but you have got to let them alone. It is just the same thing in handling your conditions.

I like this Monday-night class better than any other class I have. I feel we will accomplish more. I heard of five or six more [people] this last week who have obtained results. But, now remember this: Your ability to demonstrate in your affairs will depend absolutely upon what is in your mind now. That is cause and effect. If you are an individual who has had a big concept, if you have been handling big things, you are able to attract big things to you. Such people have the ability to put their minds to big commercial projects. It is because like attracts like and for no other reason. There is a great mental law and it is given to us to use it and we are foolish if we don't:

Remember—if you want to get a big thing, you have got to expand your consciousness so you would be able to receive a big thing if it were to come to you. Then any activity in our affairs, and in all those things, we must first enlarge our consciousness by reaching out in Mind more and more and more, realizing that we are dealing with the only power there is and then trying to feel we are connected with it and it knows and understands and receives and returns. There is always a reciprocal action between mind and that which is universal and that which is individual, and when it is flowing through you, you must realize you are dealing with a law which cannot not demonstrate. You are not taking any chance, you are not asking any questions, you are not making any supplications—no, you are not making a prayer from the ordinary standpoint of prayer. You are using a power which is and you have a right to use it and it will reach right up to your ability to use it. It is limited by our mental concept, absolutely. While it is the power that makes that planet and everything on it, it makes you and it makes me, when it comes to working in our life individually, over our conditions and over our bodies, it can only flow in through our consciousness, no other way, and what we want to do is to provide that great, big consciousness within. Make our unity with big projects, with big things, big enterprises. You can never jump away from yourself, because, don't you know? When you jump you take yourself right with you and when you land there you are. People try to jump away from themselves. People think, if I had a definite condition, if I had a definite place. You have got to provide this thing right where you are; if you are in hell, and when hell has cooled off you are ready to go somewhere else. You have got to save yourself and if the world had realized that years and years ago, the world would not need any more salvation today. Who is coming to save you? Why, God has already done it. God has done everything there is to be done. We can think of nothing better than this earth is; it is beautiful, it is lovely, it is bountiful, yet we are in the midst of plenty starving to death, in the midst of harmony yet miserable and suffering. We have all the fullness of creation and yet we live like the animals. And in a childish, weak way we blame everything on God and then think we are suffering for righteousness' sake. This is a mistake, for it is not right to suffer. It is all wrong, else we would have a suffering God which would be a monstrosity. So then, we must conclude we are suffering because we are wrong and when we harmonize with law, why, law is ready right off to be used. So then, we have got to get rid of that false concept before we can demonstrate. We have got to get rid of it. We have got to realize our unity with real life, with real things, and no longer with little personal things.

I think I get the best results when I do it this way, viewing my affairs from an absolutely impersonal standpoint. Instead of saying, I have to do this, or saying this is my work and I have this to do and I have just this much strength to put into it, we should kind of get away from our work, and let this thing be operated upon, and here we stand. The silent force of Mind flows through us and does it in an impersonal way. Then money comes to us and houses and lands. If your consciousness is right, you cannot keep them away from you. They will come and unconsciously dump right down on top of you. Jesus told the people that years ago. He said, ". . . Houses and lands will be added unto you." It is an absolute fact they will be. The ordinary person grabs at them and steps on them so that nobody will take them away. That is not the universal principle. The universal principle is flowing in and out constantly. I have come to have money, houses, and lands, and automobiles, and they are in Mind, every one of them to use. But I would not own anything in my possession that I would not willingly take out and drop and not care if I ever heard of again. I mean in the objective. It has a real scientific fact behind it, and that is the principle of circulation. Do you know, if you tie a cord around your leg so you stop circulation that your leg will die in a few hours. Everything in nature provides for a complete circuit in itself. If things are congested, they must stop.

You will find in practice what will happen is this: If instead of being so grasping, while I believe that we should always be getting, always accumulating more and more and more to the very last day we live, not to hang on to it because every consciousness should be constantly expanding. We are living in consciousness and not in conditions, so this is the way we should look at it; there is just life, and we are in it. Suppose in your practice you are seeking to demonstrate. You realize first this power flows by and all you have to do is to reach out and take it. You give direction to the law, and the law returns the thing to you. And think that is mine to use as long as I want it. I am master of that law. I say the point is this: There is the power and that power is itself impersonal and so long as we remain simply in our personality, we are not letting in that impersonal force to flow through us. So in our conditions, we should not struggle; the big things are done. If you want to attract to you great big things, if you are a little afraid they won't come, get rid of that. Get all the quieter in your consciousness. You will still be going about in the objective world attending to things just as usual, but behind it all there is a power you know is all right. It is all right and it will see the thing and it will see it done. It is wonderful the way that thing will work if you can learn to let it alone and let it. Most of us get it started and not realizing that all is Mind, or just partly realizing it, you know thought is the most subtle thing, and we disturb a demonstration with a little fear about it. We are setting some obstruction in the way, and since all is Mind and you think a little obstruction, that is the obstruction. So you must know the whole thing is done from the beginning to the end. So all the time we must be expanding our consciousness, and you have got to take time to do that. I do not know of any shortcut to do it. I do not know of any shortcut to consciousness. Consciousness has got to be developed by persistence, by endeavor, by maintaining an even temperament with yourself. You have got to be on good terms with yourself most of the time. That is not easy. There are not many people who are that way. You have got to have a great perseverance with yourself. You have to set yourself on the path again and so get along with yourself better. And let yourself have a chance. Never condemn yourself. Forgive yourself if you have done wrong. That is right. We have the power to forgive ourselves. So set yourself right and then you will find you are sailing along smoothly and you are almost there and, flop, down you go. And again you have got to do it. It does not matter how much patience it takes; it is the only thing that will win out: perseverance and patience with yourself until you can see that each succeeding month your consciousness is learning. The thing will follow in its turn. Instead of saying to my patients "How are you getting along?" I say, "Are you thinking right?" If you are neutralizing the wrong thought within, the right thought will come to you.

Now, we will take our treatment. Put everything out of your mind. This class is for conditions.

Take something that you feel your mind can encompass, something of which you have a mental cognizance within you now, and then realize that this word which you speak is surrounded by an active power which projects itself around the word, forms the thing which the word embodies and objectifies it in some way. We do not have to know the way.

In perfect calm confidence, and perfect trust in yourself, wait.

No matter how big a thing you have got, forget it. It is just as easy to demonstrate a big thing as a little one. The whole thing must be done without a sense of strain. God does not struggle; God just knows. So when we give a treatment, there should be no sense of strain or strife but only a sense of calm confidence and perfect peace which is born of that inner conviction that knows that "beside me there is none other." Since there is nothing to oppose our word, since it is the word which is all, it does not have to struggle.

We feel we are using the one power there is. We believe and know that our word which is spoken forth into this power is the law of good. Saying this here and now, we know there is nothing can hinder it.

With perfect confidence, let us each take that thing which we are working on. The treatment which I shall give is for myself and each one of you treat for yourself, and our united consciousness, or belief, strengthens everyone. I am thinking of the thing I am working on for myself, a great big thing. I feel that my consciousness is big enough to realize what it is, mine to have, that thing. I feel that my mind can give birth to it, and so I know that the word which I am speaking now is the law of this thing; I can just feel it surrounded by infinite intelligence and power. I know that this word, I can feel it, is backed up by infinite life, that the very presence of that power and life which permeates this word is enough to destroy every race consciousness that manifests, destroy every thought which is negative or which is a suggestion of limitation or lack. This word is the law of immediate activity in this thing. Realize that this is the law that says it now. It is the law of perfect harmony. There are no obstructions in the path; nothing can obstruct it, neither people, place, nor things, because none of those can intercept it. It is done now. Perfect harmony, causation. Perfect activity, Divine Intelligence is leading, guiding. That law of perfect attraction in me which is the Spirit of the Almighty in me, because I believe. I know that it is going out and drawing that thing back to me.

I know that my word is one with the Infinite Mind. I feel that that word has become a universal word. Let your consciousness go out as we realize that we are one with all life, with all people, with all things, with all Mind.

Just feel that you have passed this whole thing over to the Infinite Power and just feel that it is being taken up and done. We have no personal responsibility. And we know that beyond it all is the Infinite Intelligence and Power and Love of the Spirit. The God of all life and activity and all power and all love and all attraction, the irresistible power of the Spirit which sweeps before it everything and knows and knows all, and knows it is done.

If you are seeking anything that contradicts that principle of unfoldment of life and love, you are contradicting a universal power which, while it will bring the thing to you, might do you more damage than good. But we are none of us desiring anything that is not for good. Do not hesitate to use it for the very smallest and greatest thing in your life. It will work.

Give it attention during the week. Let yourself every day during the week demonstrate. You must do that, of course, to get the perfect concept. Keep right at it. Refuse to see the opposite thing or to have anything to do with it. Know that it will work; have absolute confidence in yourself. Be willing to do in every way, shape, and manner what you want the law to do for you. See everything right, everything perfect. Don't talk and don't talk with people on the negative side of life. Keep away from them. You cannot mix oil and water. Tell them that you do not care to discuss those things. You have more time to use when you are away from them. There are not any two ways—*and see that you demonstrate.*

Part II

Tuesday and Thursday Lectures

September and October 1918

Law

There is only one fundamental formula, one fundamental proposition, one fundamental principle, and we must always be reiterating the same thing. We do not come to a metaphysical lecture to hear something new. There is nothing new to hear. We get together to discuss the same principle, to see if we can draw something more from it which will enable us to a greater degree to use that principle. That principle itself is simplicity, yet it is infinite. It is Infinite Mind and infinite manifestation of Mind. It is a spiritual universe governing itself through thought, or the word which first becomes law, which law creates the concept of the word into what we call matter. The threefold universe of Spirit, which is the word, the creative power, or the result of the material universe in which we live. Our bodies are included in this material universe.

Jesus was a great scientific man; and as Thomas Edison was a man who discerns electrical truth about electricity, so Jesus was a man who discerned the truth about spiritual principles more than any other man who ever lived. He proclaimed the eternal reign of law, understanding, absolute, complete, perfect, and he found that law to be operative through his own thought of consciousness and so through the power of his own word. You and I must cease looking outside ourselves to any person, any place, or to any thing, and we ultimately must at last realize that whatever truth or power we have must flow through us. And when we begin to interpret our own nature, we shall begin to understand God and law and life and not until.

We have discovered this in metaphysics, that we live and move and have our being in what we call an infinite Mind, an infinite creative Mind, an infinite receptive Mind, an all-operative Mind, an omnipotent Mind, an all-knowing Mind. And we have learned that that Mind presses against us on all sides. It flows through us. It becomes operative through our thinking. We have learned that the human race, ignorant of the laws of this Mind, ignorant of the power of our own thought, has misused it through that ignorance. We have abused that creative power of thought, and the human race has brought upon itself the thing which was feared, because all thought is law and all law is Mind in action. The word which you speak today is the law which shall govern your life tomorrow as the word which you speak ignorantly or innocently, consciously or unconsciously yesterday is absolutely governing your life today. As metaphysicians, then, we are not dealing with a material universe. We are not denying a manifest universe but we are claiming that the manifestation is the result of the inner activity of the Mind and that if we want a definite manifestation we must produce a definite inner activity. You and I are not dealing with condition; we are dealing with mental law, spiritual law. We are dealing with the power of thought, the power of Mind and Spirit which knows nothing but its own power, which, from itself, without any external aid, without anything that you know or I know, takes itself

74

and makes out of itself that thing which it desires, expresses it so
we realize that the inspiration and the expression, or the cause and
the effect, are one and the same thing. We have always realized that;
we have always known that God was Spirit and that Spirit speaks
the word and the thing happens. We have prayed to this Spirit,
which is God. We have beseeched this Spirit which we call God.
We have thrown ourselves prostrate upon our faces before this
Spirit which is God. This Spirit, which is God, has not answered
our prayers and we have thought we were cursed. And the answer
did not come, and we have said, "God hears and does not please to
answer." We have never realized that perhaps God did not hear
after all, and perhaps there was no such God as we prayed to, and
that perhaps the God we prayed to did not exist at all.

Did you ever stop to realize that God is omnipresent and
knows everything like its own nature? That if God heard your
prayer and the Divine Creative Mind accepted your prayer, and if
it heard it, it would have to accept it? That because of its very omnipotence that prayer would have to be answered. It could not help
it. We have to accept the fact that the God to whom the human
race has been praying does not exist. There is no such God. It is
not sacrilegious; it is, in fact, just the opposite. It is at least turning
to the real God who knows something, and who operates in a natural, normal manner, governing everything through absolute laws.
There is no use in anybody's claiming that they have a revelation
from God, unless that revelation will prove itself as it becomes operative through some law of cause and effect. If I say God has revealed to me that I can do a certain thing, I must do that thing to
prove I have the revelation. You see what we have done? And it is
natural we should have done it. We have thought of God and
likened God to what we would be if we were God. We would get
mad, for one thing, and then everyone would have to pay. Then, we

would be pleased, and everything would be nice for a while. Then, we would fight awhile with everybody who did not agree with us. Practically every war is traced to some religious fanaticism of some kind or other. There is no such a God as that. Do you think that God fights in or for or over or against or about or around anything? Of course not. There is no god of war. You may say, "If that is true, why do we pray for victory?" We pray for victory of right, and if we are right we will win. We are not praying to slay anybody. We are not fighting the people of any particular country. We are fighting the false thought that manifests through a government, and it will be destroyed and its embodiment will go with it. There is no such thing as a God of struggle and war, and all such ideas are old and untrue. These ideas find their way into our literature, our art, more or less into everything.

Jesus came to reveal a different god: "I come to fulfill the law," to teach you that which the prophets perceived. And "Go ye and do likewise." Everything is governed by law. The law is written in our own hearts, and we are governed by law. Moses saw law in the universal aspect. I do not know how, but he discovered that we are surrounded by an infinite law which was a law of cause and effect, which was a law which existed—"an eye for an eye, and a tooth for a tooth"—which would compel us to obey it as a universal force. Moses did not know anything about a God of love. Moses was an old heathen, according to our idea of right and wrong. Ungodlike concepts of God—and we build our church on such a concept. No wonder it falls. A concept of a God who slays and murders and burns. Moses saw the law just about as it is. He saw the law of cause and effect, and how it gives back to us what we put out. That has become the foundation of all law of civilization since then. It is because that law Moses saw was universal truth. It will grind you to powder. And it operates through our thought, and we use this law as we think.

Jesus came and did not take anything away from the law; he did not try to change the law. He said, "I come not to destroy but to fulfill the law." Jesus personified the impersonal law, revealed beyond the law the word and the infinite spirit of mercy and understanding and then revealed the Spirit and taught that it works through the human instrument. I am the manifestation of this intelligence. What is true of God is true of me. Whatever I see God doing I can do. And Jesus raised the dead, and he healed the blind and the crippled. And they said he must be God or he could not do it. So they said Jesus was God and believed it; and it has been good for the human race, and whatever has come out of it has been good.

We should not look back; we should look forward. The church was a good institution years ago, the church of the Dark Ages—when humanity did all those murderous things—was good. The church was necessary then because people did not have sense. But now, as fast as people have sense they get out of that idea for the need of church. It should not be condemned or supported by anybody. The thing it stood for, the thing it supported, the concept has been swept away, and there remains nothing but a shell.

So it is with many of our educational institutions, with many of our scientific concepts; they are errors, shells of what people once thought. Now we have an entirely different concept. Jesus revealed to us, and because he discerned spiritual law and knew it was operative through us, the power of that law was with him.

Let us consider the modern things. Jesus healed all manner of sickness in its worst forms. There is not a disease known to the human race which has not been healed through the principles of the religion we teach, but what was healed? It takes us time to arrive at an understanding for a healing to take place.

We were given a "rush order" to give a treatment for a particular woman. That woman was brought right out of the grave because she was in a dying condition. I remember that everyone present got a wonderful realization, which is a tremendous power. Such a thing as that compares very favorably with the centurion who went to Jesus and asked him to send out the word.

I would not be surprised at anything. I am trying to train my mind so I will not be surprised if things should appear right out of the air. It is law and we have as much of it as we can realize, truly accept. Take the Bible story of Jesus bringing a boat immediately to the shore. I have never tried to explain it. I just suppose it was. We can never experience a manifestation until we internally know something that could correspond to it in our experience. You only know what you know. I used to think I knew, but now I know I know what I know or learn. When I experienced something myself where I saw one physical body brought from quite a distance, I knew that Jesus with his understanding had caused the boat to immediately come to the shore. And whether it really did happen or not, he was obeying the law.

We say Jesus must have been God, because he materialized something out of the air. I believed it because I was brought up to believe the Bible. But I didn't **know** that Jesus materialized substance out of the air. I used to reason it out. I tried to imagine Jesus as walking through a wall, and I used to think that he walked right straight through it. I believed it because the Bible said so. And somewhere or other it was law, it was truth, it was the power that always governs truth and law and Jesus came and touched the "hem" of truth and law. He put the effect where people could reach it. He taught this: There is the kingdom of heaven within, a kingdom of spirit which governs itself through the power of the word. And he located it within himself and within everybody and throughout the vast reaches of space. It was omnipresent. The God of everywhere operated through the law which is written in our hearts, and moreover, he said, "I am," and whenever we say "I am," we are proclaiming the law of life. If I say "I am sick," there is nothing to hinder my being sick if I proclaim it long enough.

Beyond it all, around and through it all, there is an infinite power that makes the law operate. We have discovered what that law is. The reason why we have discovered that law absolute, that we claim it to be a science, is this: Everything in the universe is a combination of thought operating through mind. It is certain because when we get the right combination of thought in our minds, it always corresponds. We say it is a religion if you want to call it that, because we realize this, because the more spiritual the thought the higher the manifestation. The more our reliance upon what we call God, the greater the power. Is it any wonder we say it is the new church as well as the new science? It is the new education because it strips all the false from the old and reveals the individual. It is the new age because as sure as God is, it shall usher in, or express, the perfect life, the revelation of this truth and our ability to use it. And when you know this and do not prove it, it is your own fault. If, knowing the infinite power flowing through you, you still remain sick and unhappy and miserable and poor, my friend, it is your own fault, and don't blame God and do not blame another person, and don't blame the devil. It is your own fault. Every time you say *I am* you are recognizing the eternal, infinite presence of omnipotent power within yourself, which is God, operating through that which you call your mind. Every time you say *I am*, it is immediately supported and you cannot say a word or think a thought that is not omnipotent. And that is why you bring upon yourself the thing you fear and why you bring to yourself the thing you want. When 51 percent of your thinking is health and life and power, that day that 51 percent will swallow up and erase [the other 49 percent]. The day you as an individual by 51 percent of thought pass beyond this perception of limitation, everything in the universe is yours and you become it. That day poverty will desert you and you will be emancipated forever. The day 51 percent of your thinking is happy, misery shall depart and never return. It is then worth your time and your effort and your aim to demand the greatest purpose in the life of any awakened soul to so depict this principle that first they shall emancipate themselves. And if you are emancipated yourself, that is all the emancipation you shall need. If I would have the courage to put on an old shirt and come down here to speak in shirtsleeves, I am emancipated. But little can be done in awakening another soul. The way can be shown, but every individual has got to take the first step. We are so bound by suggestion, so hypnotized by false belief, so wound and entangled by the chaotic thinking of the world which is based upon the principle of a dual mind; we are so confused, that we are not ourselves. Now, wake up! Your word is all-powerful. Your consciousness is one with omnipotence. Your thought is infinite. Your destiny is eternal and your home is everlasting heaven. And all that ever was or is or ever shall be is now the truth and never was changed and never will be. This is the way for you and me to think, and we shall begin from this day our emancipation.

I first realize the truth. I am living in a perfect universe; it always was perfect and always will be perfect. There never was a mistake made. There are no mistakes being made. And there never will be any mistakes made. This will contradict everything you have experienced and because of thought, all that which seems to be a mistake, which seems to be imperfect, which our carnal mind has suffered from is a false concept. Being false it is a coward and flees before the truth which I have just spoken. It destroys it from my consciousness forever and sets my consciousness safe in a new light and a new life and a new realization, and I say my word is the infinite activity of the Almighty and that it knows itself to be the infinite activity of the Almighty, and it could not come forth with any more power. It is just as much the word of God as any word spoken by God. Now, believe it. *It is.* There is only one that is, one word, one mind. Then that person who believes in sickness, and sinning and limited and poor and filled with the suggestion and the race environment, and the so-called laws of inheritance, realize it is a delusion and a lie, and there is no truth in these beliefs. They never did exist. It is such a lie that my consciousness does not know it exists.

I am one with the Infinite Intelligence that makes things out of itself and is not governed by the thing which it has made. The clay cannot reply to the potter that molds it, and I am the molder of my own life backed up by an infinite power. And that which says that a person is poor is nothing but a hypnotic thought, and I do not believe it. We stand in the midst of eternal life. But as long as you claim less, you will get less. You will get what you ask for. *I am that I am, and beside me there is none other. I am the power of attraction within thee.* So I set myself free.

I have no physical body; that which calls itself a physical body is an illusion. I have a spiritual body here and now. Know that the law of atomic theory that says that we are made of dust and must return to it and that race suggestion that says it is true, is a lie.

Mind is eternal activity; it needs no rest, it needs no sleep. I am the power of infinite peace. I am sufficient unto myself. I am one with all that is, one with every person that is, one in eternal union with the All That Is. This word that I speak is the truth, the whole truth and nothing but the truth, forever. I am manifesting, forever, full and free.

That is the way for you to think about yourself. That is the way to use the law. And that is the way to speak it forth.

The Law
and the Word

In metaphysics, as in everything else, we are dealing with a proposition which is the substance of things which are not seen by the physical eye. The human eye sees only that which is effect; the human hand touches only that which is effect; and we are very apt to say these effects are controlled by law. That is true; everything must be governed by law. Law controls everything, absolutely. But we are not as apt to realize that the law itself is an effect. Did you ever stop to think that not only is this planet an effect, that is, this planet did not make itself, it is an effect? When you do, you will see it is governed by law and made by law, but that law which governs this planet is also an effect. The law did not make itself. The law is not intelligence, as causation, it is the result of intelligence as causation, and that brings us back, and we say then, what is the cause?

As metaphysicians we claim that the word is the cause, the word is the cause of the law, and the law is the cause of the thing and the thing is the effect of the law and the law is the effect of the word. It means this in practice: that the law is written into our own hearts and that we speak the word and the word creates the law and the law governs the thing.

The word was with God and the word was God, and the word still is God. Our word, our thought, is the activity of that one Mind in our consciousness; the thing that holds the planet in its place; the thing that causes your blood to circulate and your food to digest, the thing that causes your business to succeed, the thing that makes the tide come in and go out, the thing that holds the planets in space is all the same thing. It is one and the same thing, but each separate thing is governed by an individual law. Each separate thing. There is a law of the buttercup. There is a law of the bean. There is a law that makes the sun shine. There is a law that makes the plant grow. There is a law that makes the wind blow, and a law that makes your heart beat. Each law is an individual law created for the specific purpose of doing that special thing. You can see then that that law is a creation of something that is higher than the law and the law cannot help itself. It is coming to see that law is the result of intelligence, it is to come into understanding of your ability to use the word which substantiates the law and makes you realize that the word you speak is the law unto the thing about which you speak it, and just as far as you come to realization. That would be realization causeless causation. You and I first realize effect, and we see we live in a world of matter. We are bound by matter or controlled by conditions. Then we say that the buttercup did not make itself, there is a law behind the buttercup. There is a law behind my life, and we see that we live in a world of law. Everything is a law of law. Law is cause and effect. That is true. We think, now I have arrived, but you will find this is still limited by the law. There is a law that says anything that is heavier than air will stay on the earth. You say, I am governed by that law, but you will find that another law transcends that law and completely annihilates it. Few people realize this, that the law did not make itself. If you think clearly and deeply enough, you will realize that without intelligence there could be no law. Don't forget that, without intelligence, there could be no law. And law is simply intelligence operating.

Intelligence, that thing which creates the law, is that thing which is without causation. We do not see it. It is without beginning and without end; it is causeless causation. It is all intelligence and knows itself to be nothing but that which it is, and now it speaks. We say it speaks of itself or says the word, and that is the result. The word is law, but the word is only a secondary cause. The word could not be spoken unless there was the intelligence that could speak it. Place the word where it belongs. The word is the thing which holds the matter in its place—what we call matter. But behind the word is the causeless cause which can make the word out of itself. It does not have to have anything before it.

So we are living in this threefold world of matter, word, cause; or the real sequence is this: cause, word, matter. I do not know of any simpler way to say it.

All the human race needs is to be taught so everybody will know how to use the word, so everybody will know they are creative centers unto themselves. This is all they need.

This causeless cause, that which is without any reason for being except that it is—that is all we know about it. Speak the word and the word becomes the concept, or the law, which produces the thing. That is the way everything is brought into being. Without the word nothing could happen, but without intelligence there could not be any word. So the beginning of everything is intelligence, causeless intelligence, limitless causation, and it begins to speak. Now we have the Infinite One manifesting itself into a manifestation of ideas.

We see that in the universe every separate idea has a word or a concept behind it, and as long as that word or concept exists the idea will exist in the visible world. When that concept is withdrawn the idea melts—physically speaking, disappears. It ceases to vibrate to the word, which is the law behind it, and when the word is withdrawn the condensation of the ether in the matter is withdrawn and the thing disappears. When the word, or your word of life, says there is no longer life in my body, it withdraws itself, or withdraws the word, and your body disintegrates; it goes back into what it came from. There is no longer any power; there is no longer anything in your body to vibrate to the thing which held it because it has been withdrawn.

The Word is God. All things were made by the Word and without the Word not anything was made that is made. You see the Word is the idea behind everything, the law that substantiates that thing. The Word is Intelligence operating upon itself always. And now that becomes a law and the law holds the thing in place so long as the word exists. That would not mean anything to you or to me if it is only a power that some god has outside ourselves. It would not mean anything to us. It does not mean anything to my life to know that God has the power to speak the word if it is external to me. What could it mean to me? Something that is nothing. But everybody who has arrived at an understanding is claiming this. Whatever we discover to be true about God I am at the same time realizing to be a truth about myself. Whatever I find to be a truth about myself, expanding my consciousness, I realize that it is a universal truth. Herein is the mystery of life. You and I are intelligent centers using the creative word for that which we will constructively or destructively, and that creative word which we use becomes the law unto the thing whereunto it is sent and becomes the concept behind it and projects the thing, creates the thing in our life. And so it might be said of my life that I am the word and without the word is not anything made into my life that is made, and the word was with me and the word was me. Absolutely everything in my life. That is a new way of looking at life, but it is absolute truth. We cannot help it; we cannot get away from it. Moreover, without my word nothing is made in my life and all things that are in my life were made by my word whether I know it or not. Because of that very fact therein lies your very divinity, and otherwise you would not be divine. You can be mechanical like a blade of grass. But we have been given the ability to choose the word we speak, and therein lies our very limitation. It is simply the misuse of our divine nature, the abuse of it, the lack of knowing that our word is cause, the ignorance that has caused us to speak a negative word. And because the word is the concept and the concept is the thing and the thing is the word itself, that word has created a negative condition. To change that negative condition I have got to use a different word, but the same cause, intelligence, and speak my word. That is the way healing is done, a demonstration made. And no living soul who is intelligent enough to walk up and down the street doubts.

I never meet anybody anymore who doubts it. There is no thinking person on the face of the earth who doubts what I am saying, because every thinking person knows there has got to be a cause for everything. People everywhere have either been healed or have known of someone who was healed or have learned of demonstrations being made. So what we want to do is to find out as nearly as we can what makes it work.

If you are a center of causation operating through the word, that word is every word you speak—*every word*. And every word you speak transcends law and creates law as fast as it goes along. There is a thing that is very hard to conceive. I took about two years studying that to see how that could be, that my word makes a new law and that new law will do a new thing. And since I am a center in causation and can think and say a word—and speak to it and it will create the law that will substantiate the word—that mighty concept of the vitality of the power behind the thing and within the thing will manifest as long as the word exists. If that is not true, all that is taught of metaphysics would be false. Since it is true, all that is taught is a practical application of law through the creative power within us or our spoken word audibly or inaudibly expressed. When you say "I am poor," you are creating the very thing that makes you poor. When you say "I am poor," you are using a word to make you poor. If you can awake to this truth, it will be the greatest truth you ever realized.

When you say "I am not poor, I am perfect in expression," whatever it is you want your word to be it is. You are using a power that nothing can withstand outside of God. That concept is all that we need. Get the concept of the creative word flowing through us to such a degree that nothing can withstand it; and that individual who can appreciate it to the greatest extent is the one who believes it. Consider the life of Jesus. He said about his word, "The word I speak unto you, it is Spirit, it is life"—that word I am saying now. He said, "My word shall never pass away till it fulfills itself; heaven and earth shall pass away but my word shall not." If we had that same conviction, it would be done. The power was and is in the word. It is all intelligence without limitation because it finds its source in a causeless causation. Can you conceive of real causation? There is no limit, since it can image anything that it wants to.

The same word we use unconsciously all the time, every time we speak, every time we think, we are using in ignorance and unconsciously. What we have to do is not a strange or peculiar thing.

It is to realize this and to begin to use the word constructively the way we want it, speaking the word for what we want and getting what we speak the word for. But can't you see that since the word is first, if you say "My body is wasting away," it will waste away? It cannot help it. The body does not act; it is always acted upon. Conditions do not act. Everything in this universe that you and I see is the result of the activity of intelligence always and the word is the cause, and the law is the medium through which the word operates to produce the effect. And you do not, and I do not care about the law or the effect if we can get the causation.

Our word will manifest at the level of our recognition, at the level of our consciousness. My word will be as big as I am conscious of life within myself. If I have a grand, an exalted concept, I have a grand, and exalted, word. Your prosperity is not a thing of condition; your prosperity is not a thing of law over which you have no control. Your prosperity depends upon the grandeur of your thought and nothing else. Your word is the cause of all that is. But few people realize that, even among those who are seeking to realize it, and we are constantly, we are constantly allowing ourselves to come under a condemnation of the race belief and believing in it and accepting that we are controlled by it.

Here is another thing: Our word has only the force we put into it. You and I are dealing with an infinite power within and without, and we have as much of it as we believe and as we speak forth with absolute conviction. But do you know that to become absolutely convinced is to become absolutely sure that the negative does not exist and that there is nothing but the positive—that there is nothing but that which knows and so long as we recognize the negative we are not recognizing the positive? What you and I want to do is to plunge very deeply into a conscious union with that infinite power. Now, we cannot do that while we believe in the opposite extreme of the power. Ultimately speaking, there is no such thing as a negative power. There is an active and a passive principle; but a positive and negative power would neutralize each other, and zero would be the result. There is but one power operating at the level of the consciousness of your life and my life. And from itself by the power of its own word it creates this planet, our bodies, and every time we speak and think we are using it. The Bible says the word is in your own mouth, that you should know it and do it. How little we do realize that, and how little any of us think and speak the way we ought to. I know in my life just what hinders me from using that word. I look myself in the face and see myself. I know what must be eliminated before there will be a greater conception. I am seeking always to do it. Do that; try to look at yourself. There is not one person in a thousand—yes, in ten thousand—who has the courage to do it. If you will do that, you will find that you have a tremendous power within yourself. There is nothing on earth that could convince me any other way. But everybody has got to know it for themselves. I can't know it for you. God already knows it for you, and you have got to accept it.

Evil is not the absence of good; it is not the lack of good; it is not inverted good; it is not good turned wrong side out. Evil is simply the absence of the recognition on the part of the individual of perfection. Don't do anything with it. Let it alone and it will swallow itself up. Anything that is unlike good or God cannot exist very long.

What shall we do with the great affirmative factor, the great affirmation? We must use it to eliminate doubt first. Whatever tendency there is in my life to doubt the ability of my word I am going to get rid of. It has got to be done however long it takes. And whatever is done is done for all time. I believe if people die sick, they are sick; if they die poor, they are poor. The body ceases but consciousness continues, and it is consciousness that is real and the body is nothing but the manifestation of it. That is why it ceases. We must awaken to the fact that we are mental beings, that we have to work out the problems of being, and the object of it all is that we raise our consciousness to the idea we are perfect. We do not have to wait. The world has gone through a long evolutionary process, but it has arrived. Believe me, we have arrived. We are there. There is nowhere else to go.

The journey has been far and long, but we have reached the goal and we have stopped right where we began—within ourselves. It is the center of the word, the center of causation, the center of law and order. People who realize that Mind governs their life by that word for them will comply with the necessities of the case, since all is law. Since our word creates always, it stands to reason that we have got to be very careful in sowing the seed. You cannot contradict nature and get an affirmative result. You cannot mix up thought, negative, and positive and get a steady stream of affirmative consciousness and results. Your consciousness, your creative power, is limited to the amount of belief you have, the word you accept. If you believe you are living in an imperfect universe, it is imperfect to you. God has not erred. God has not made a mistake. There is nothing wrong. That which we called wrong will soon pass away and leave only that which is right, and you and I are all right, the universe is all right, and everybody is all right. Until you believe that, most of the volume of your consciousness will be negative behind it. If everything is all right, *everything is all right.* But if you think people are all wrong and you are all wrong and everything is all wrong, it will be all wrong to you. You cannot mix up things. For illustration I like to think of taking a tubful of clear water. I remember my mother would put bluing in the wash water. Now we use bleach, which is clear in color. Notice if you put only a drop of bluing in one corner of the tub, it blues the whole tub-ful of water. You better be careful what you are thinking. If you are negative in one area of your thinking, it affects all areas of your life. There must be but one thing in consciousness, truth.

Do not strain; that implies doubt and is a negative power. All you have to do is to know it. To struggle to concentrate is to sup-pose that you have to condense at one point universal power, when it is always at every point. Do get over all these things that imply strain and enjoy, for that loosens up your consciousness and makes things come easy to you.

In joy, peace, happiness, realization and of course the highest word, produce the highest effect. That person whose idea of God and her relationship to God is most exalted, most companionable and inspirational, and realizing the infinity of her own self, would not hesitate to speak. It will not take away from you a God; it will give you a real God. It will resurrect the savior of your conscious-ness. The one who gets the most exalted idea when speaking the word, may say, "It is not my word, it is the word of all, it is eternal and ever operative and it cannot fail." The whole thing is put right out into the Divine, the whole impulse of love will bring about an answer. You will find that such people begin to live in a different world. They are no longer subject to conditions, they are no longer subject to effects. They know that their word is immediately cre-ative, it is immediately law. If it is a new word, it is a new law. It is immediately operative and manifesting, and it will do new things unto them. We will in time come back to find that the word is in our own mouths. We will find that we, ourselves, individually, do the writing. You are each a law unto yourselves. Become unto your-selves a law of happiness, a law of peace, a law of health, life, love, truth, and beauty, and go forth to radiate that which you feel your-self to be. It is the only salvation that will ever come to this world.

Everything else has been tried and has proved a miserable and utter failure. Insofar as you and I and everybody thinks the word, uses it, and makes it their word, we are perfecting ourselves and are becoming true saviors to the human race. That is your duty and it is mine, to every day prove this word in our life, for it is the great reality. Your word is the law unto the thing. You declare that this word you are speaking is the law unto this situation. It cannot be added to or taken away from. That is what makes it work. The bigness of that thing, all the reality of it, all the advantage of it. All the life of it. Know that we will be able to do it. It is my desire that everybody who reads this will first realize that the word is in them.

Divine Science

There is a mental and a spiritual side to life. We live in a threefold existence—mental, physical, and spiritual. All three are real or they would not be, but to live in any one to the exclusion of the other two is a mistake. If you live purely in the physical, you become simply an animal; if you live only in the mental, you become simply intellectual; if you live merely in the spiritual, you are very apt to evaporate in sentiment. The normal person has a normal activity in all three. Spirit is realized as cause, mind as intelligence and law, and physical or matter, is the result of the activity of spirit through mind. So it is normal to understand, study, and use all three planes of existence.

Let us now consider the spiritual. Previously we discussed the mental aspect of the law more than the spiritual. And it is the mental aspect of the law, that mental understanding of the law of cause and effect, of the power of the word and our ability to use it that is our ability to demonstrate to a large degree. It is perhaps to the mind as it belongs to the spiritual side of life to get that inner essence, that inner feeling that gives life to our word, that real sense of the unity of the spirit in us. A real companionable, reciprocal feeling about God. The human soul has always believed in God; therefore, a god must exist. We are finding this God resides in us, speaks through us but it is nevertheless God, just the same. We are not in metaphysics doing away with God, we are bringing God into our lives. We are just learning about God. Instead of seeing God as afar off, God is right within. That is all the difference between our God and the most orthodox God you ever heard of. This God is within and is universal, flowing through everything, an impersonality. But it is still a God of intelligence, a God of understanding, and of power. And so there is something which is beyond your consciousness and mind which causes us to do what we do, the Spirit. We call it being led of the Spirit. The old Quakers believed that. They were much more spiritual, much nearer the truth than any other denomination. They at least sought, or waited for, the leading of the Spirit within their lives, and they always expected to find it within themselves.

There is something right within you and within me that is awaiting expression, and what we must learn to do is to get out of the way and let it express itself. Withdraw to ourselves, receive and distribute this Spirit. There is an infinite desire seemingly on the part of this Spirit to express itself, to become something and I find that we do things, largely, not because we always care to but because we must. I speak because I must, I teach because I must, I treat because I must, not because I desire to. There are a thousand things I would rather do. I would rather be a farmer. It is a great deal more pleasurable to work in the garden than it is to give a lecture. People become metaphysicians because their soul has arrived to the consciousness that they are no longer looking outside of themselves for that I-am-ness; and for the individual who realizes that there is an irresistible impulse to express it. People who become metaphysicians on any other basis have not got the working power behind them. If you feel that way, you will interpret everything through this power behind you. People say to me, "Why do you have such big classes? Why do such large crowds come?" It is the power behind the thing. I know that I work with a tremendous power. Now it is not personal with me; it is just as impersonal to me as if I were a blackboard. I do not make people come. That would be a limited concept. There is a power that operates wherever you might be that does everything. We say it is Spirit. We have that Spirit within ourselves. This is where we differ from other people. We are not different from them in reality. Someday they will do the same thing because they will have to. Back of your word and back of my word and back of our objective life there is a great power that is doing something. It knows what it wants, it knows why it wants it, and knows how to get it. And the spiritual side of metaphysics is our consciousness to let that power operate through us, to let the Spirit come forth into our word. But before we can do that, we must ourselves destroy that which is unlike God.

Never forget this—God does not make evil; we make all that we experience of evil, and since we make it we have got to unmake it. It is something that contradicts life; life cannot produce death. Take this war, for instance. God did not make this war; God will never unmake this war. Since God did not make it, we might pray forever and it would not stop the war if we were to pray to God to stop it. If that kind of prayer would stop it, it would be stopped. All the civilized world is praying for the war to stop, whether they call themselves Christians or not. There is a ceaseless prayer going *up* to what we call God. We do not care who it is that is praying, and if God hears and if God answers, and God must hear if it is God, the war would stop. We made the war and we have got to finish it ourselves. This is reasonable, and God plays no part in it whatever. That must be true, or there is not truth on earth. God does not work destructively. That should teach us this lesson and, believe me, it is the lesson it is teaching the world this minute and it will change the whole philosophy of the world. They will have an entirely different sort of God after this war is over, an entirely different God. Have you read some of the new literature since this war began? Especially by Wells? He is writing a new article in the *Republic*, a new book. In this story is a man who is supposed to meet God and asks questions, and God says, "Let men settle that among themselves; that is man's business."

People are changing their minds about God. And so we are compelled to state the fact that evil is the creation of our own false consciousness, and since it is, it is useless to pray to God to stop evil. We have got to stop evil. God is good and complete and perfect. Evil will only destroy itself.

Since that is true, on the spiritual side of metaphysics we do not recognize evil at all. We just claim that evil is the great unreality, the great race illusion, the great not-understanding but the great misunderstanding, the great mistake and we must cease doing evil and begin to do that which is good. That is all we have got to do. And immediately when we do it, and if it is done by a nation it will be the same, or if it is done by an individual. Let any individual or nation cease thinking evil and begin to think and do only that which is good, and right off they will find that they have a power that is complete. And now that is known to us. I just call it the power. I know there is that power. If I were to go to a new city or town, a power would go with me. Of course, it is there before I go, but from the standpoint of personally speaking, I say it would go with me. And through that power a crowd would gather wherever I spoke, and everybody in that city I had a message for would come. I do not know how it would do it, but there is a power that would do it. I would know the same thing if I were in business. It is power that does it all. It is something behind it that knows the beginning and the middle and the end; it knows the end from the beginning. It knows everything.

The reason that you and I have hindered this power in this life is because of our individuality. When we first awakened to consciousness on this plane, we ceased to progress mechanically. Up until the time we awoke to consciousness, the power compelled us to evolve. You can see how that would be, can't you? We had not awakened yet to our own divine consciousness and recognized our own individuality. We had not evolved to where we could wake up to it. It was a long, long time ago. It was when we first arose from the earth, if we did, and knew that we were self-conscious individuals. And from that minute, the power ceased to mechanically work. Is that clear? Don't be afraid to admit that it is not clear if it is not. It means that all the power has ever done or ever can do in our evolution it has already done, and whatever is going to be done from now on, and whatever has been done from the moment of self-consciousness recognized in the individual we have got to let be done through us. Ever since we knew ourselves, we have governed ourselves as we chose. We have murdered, hated, stolen, et cetera. Take the life of any nation—the United States—they decided to become a nation. Nothing said I will or I won't. There is always a power ready to help those who harmonize with it. They chose to have a civil war among themselves. God did not come down and say, "Look here, that won't do." God just let them fight. The world arises today and begins to fight. There is no reason on earth for it, absolutely none. There is reason for our being in the war but no reason for the war in the beginning, just a belief that there is not enough in the world for everybody. God did not say to

Germany, "You shall not fight," nor to Belgium, nor to England, nor France, et cetera, et cetera. God did not come down and say, "This will never do. This is bad." God just let them fight. And see how they fight! We are compelled to believe that we do it ourselves, and this is the secret of all life. We do it ourselves because we are individuals. You and I will never progress one inch farther while the same Power, that is God, is pressing against our consciousness for a further unfoldment of Itself through us, a greater self-recognition in us. You and I objectively have got to decide what that will is. And therein lies our divine individuality, and the absolute proof of it that God can express through us only as far as we will manifest. Here is the Power and here I am and if I am working with the Power, it knows the thing from the beginning. It knows how to do the thing because it has done it so far. The Spirit of Truth in me has done everything so far. And now it desires my recognition. That is what Jesus said: "Behold, I stand at the door and knock." All the power there is stands outside of our divine individuality and waits that we shall know it

The spiritual side of this science in no way departs from the law and the word. It still recognizes the necessity of law or still recognizes that law is created from the word and matter is created from the law. But it seeks to embody in that word such an amount of the spirit of truth that the word will never misrepresent reality and consequently the appearance in the outer will always be true. When the human race will learn that thought, there will be no more sickness. When the human race with consciousness says and believes that, evil will cease to exist. It will disappear. It will be neutralized when 51 percent of the human race says and believes that, because the majority will be on the side of Light. Until that time every individual must of necessity be more or less bound by what we call race consciousness. You and I cannot perfectly emancipate ourselves from the human race consciousness until the whole race consciousness is emancipated from itself. That is why many of us who are in truth still have many things to work out. It is all impersonal. Jesus himself could not do it. Jesus suffered. That is how we suffer from the sins of the race. We are all in a consciousness that the human race has fulfilled, and we all more or less believe in. We should so penetrate the reality of God. We must come to the point where we recognize ourselves going to the center. God is flowing through us. We are not a projection of God; something came forth from God. We are not a reflection of God which is just an insubstantial image. You and I must come to realize that we are a center of this God-conscious operation and activity. And when we realize that, we will find that within us there is the Spirit that seeks harmony, within us and not without. You know that when you meet a specially gifted person. I was talking with somebody the other day who plays the piano very beautifully. She is a professional woman and so she has little time to play the piano, and she had to leave it alone entirely for several years. When she did have a few moments she could give to her music, it seemed as if something would tear her open. Such an urge! Why? Because her consciousness was very thin to it. The veil was thin between real music and her expression of it. It is the Divine Urge in anybody. It is the thing that makes the singer sing. Mechanical singing is nothing. It is soul. It is the thing that makes an actor always act. Sarah Bernhardt could not quit. If there was nothing left but skin and bone, she would not have quit acting because the Spirit was so pronounced. Do not think it is anything but the Spirit because there is nothing but the Spirit to act and it was acting through her, and that is what does it. That is what makes a person write a book, or preach a sermon. It is that Spirit which will express itself. And now, it is within us. That Spirit is in every living thing, is in every soul, latent, simply waiting to be brought forth and come through the avenue we express. It is to bring out these great realities of life and happiness, health, love, and power, to supply these things that make life worthwhile. Life is created through us and we are manifested through God in order that the Supreme Spirit which feels itself to be full of lovingness shall express itself in outward form and that is the way we have the body and that is the way the body is becoming more perfected, until we become a perfect image through which to manifest God. We are that body of God, but we don't know it as yet. You and I have within us that thing which is going to manifest itself and as we more and more open our consciousness, turning within to the greater creating lovingness and express in our life a greater joy, happiness, strength, power, a greater individuality, no matter what line it may be along, it is simply one thing doing it, the Power. It is God that wants to do it. It is not the human you or the human me at all. There is not any human you and human me. There is only the Divine One which flows through all, expresses that concrete individuality. These things are true, but until we recognize them they do not become true to us; but let the individual turn within and there is the Power of the Spirit ready, and because of this divine individuality it never would express without recognition. So we have got to recognize it.

That is the process that Jesus went through at the tomb of Lazarus. He recognized the supremacy of the power. He said, "If you believe, you will see the glory of God." What did he do? He recognized God, Spirit, as the only power that is. He said, "I know you always hear me." Then he spoke the truth. We must begin to recognize that behind it all there is an Infinite Spirit. The Spirit of Christ is the recognition of this God-consciousness operating through the individual and using it for the unfoldment of God.

Unless we get an understanding that we control by the spirit of good, we have a very dangerous weapon. But no matter how tremendous our power of mind is, if we still control by the spirit of good, it is the spirit of Christ, and we can never misuse it. That is why I always think—feel about my work—that there is something greater than I am, greater than I know myself humanly to be. It is not greater than my real spirit. My real spirit is its manifestation, but I in the Spirit am greater than I know myself to be in the external. There is something behind all life, flowing through everything that is expressing itself in everything. In the mechanical universe it does it mechanically, in the planet, in the plant. The plant is fed and clothed without any effort. The same thing is in us. It would feed and cloth us harmoniously, govern our life, keep our body well and strong, and preserve our youth forever; but our own divine individuality has come in and not let our real nature assert itself. That is why when we have a desire, we have a right to speak that word. It is the very power and presence of the Almighty.

When you speak the word of truth for anybody, you must not feel that it is a poor word. Realize that it is going to manifest. It is the presence and power of the Infinite which has the power of life within itself to express itself. All you have to do is to speak it and know that the power of the Spirit does it unto you. Thus let us learn more and more we are having a higher degree of manifestation, as we are coming to see that all error is impersonal. It is simply false thought operating through people. Truth is impersonal. It is true thought. We are dealing only with thought and with nothing else. As we realize the spiritual truth, everything else will take care of itself because it becomes causeless cause, a law unto the life of that person for whom we speak the word for their body and their conditions. God is in everybody; everybody has that power for themselves. All there is of you is God. All the real you that there is, is some activity of God in you because there is nothing else it could be. But we have not recognized it, therefore we have not had it to use. All we have got to do is to recognize it. This will give power to our word. It is simplicity itself. It is not any hard thing to do. You recognize—you say, "I speak this word, I give this treatment, I have no responsibility for it." The treatment itself is the law of God asserting itself to be that which is. Consequently, humanly speaking, it annuls every man-made law, because it is the higher law swallowing up the lower.

Manifestation is not the balancing of two opposing forces. If it was, it would mean that evil equals good, which is an absolute impossibility. Evil equals nothing when good is present. If it equals something, it would have reality and life in it and there would be a destructive force. Jesus said, "A house divided against itself cannot stand." Evil amounts to zero and zero never equals one. Never forget that. If good comes in, evil goes out. It cannot help it. It cannot stay. We in a certain sense think evil is a negative thought force; it seems to have a kind of personality. Evil seems to try to destroy good, but it cannot. It is that impersonal evil, that negative destructive power of thought that makes people sick. It is a race suggestion. You see what it is doing? It is operating on people's bodies because they believe it. You let any person arise with the reality of spiritual power and know that it annuls that human law and it could not affect that person. It could not remain in that consciousness any more than darkness can remain in a lighted room. I do not know where it came from or goes to. Where does sickness go? It came from a false belief that mind is in matter divorced from God and that we are separate from our Creator and subject to conditions. Therefore false ideas have produced sickness. Let us believe the opposite, knowing, understanding that

God is in us, that God *is*, and that love, truth, and power are within us. We are the very substance of the Infinite itself; our body is the substance of Spirit itself, and we won't be sick. Where our consciousness is permeated with 51 percent of right thinking, we are healed. When there is more light brought into this room than there is darkness, the darkness will disappear. It will cease to exist. That is our process.

Daily we must come to that inner power which is greater than the outer power. Daily we must come to the inner spirit within us which is greater than our conditions. Do not seek to find God away off somewhere. You will never do it. Stop right where you are and realize that God is within you operating everything—the spirit and life essence of everything—and wait right there for that power to manifest itself into conviction. And then you begin to create your word which sets in motion the law which produces the thing for you, and you will find that you will be surprised at the power of your word. It becomes the very activity and power of the Infinite.

Take a few minutes now to recognize the Spirit of Truth within you. That is what you must awake to before you can use the law. Forget everything else as you recognize God within.

Let us realize that Spirit is Intelligence and Power; it is health, happiness, peace and prosperity, supply and activity—it is the consciousness of the complete and perfect life.

Declare that this day there is perfect life come forth from you—perfect healing. That which is perfect is complete.

Realize perfect manifestation this day over all conditions. Realize that the Power which is infinite is flowing through and manifesting.

Feel yourself satisfied—at perfect peace.

We know that the word which we have created here is the presence and activity and the power of the Spirit of all life, and as such we declare that it is infinite and eternal and operative, omnipotent and All, and it shall work until it perfectly fulfills Itself, and we know that that word is.

Let us believe this word goes with us forever.

The Law

of Attraction

I think sometimes we do not quite realize or recognize the absoluteness of law, and we do not recognize quite clearly enough that all law is cause and effect; nothing can happen in the outside unless there is something corresponding to it on the inside of life. Everything that comes to us comes through a law of attraction. You could not draw anything to you until there was first an avenue for that thing, through which that thing could flow toward you. You could not draw riches to you if you held the thought of poverty; you could only draw more of the same thing—more poverty. That is why Jesus said, "When you pray, believe that you have and you shall receive." They were to first provide within themselves the mental pattern of the thing prayed for. That person who can provide the best mental pattern—that is what we call realizing—that one who can do it the best, gets the best results. But we are all filled with some kind of a mental pattern. There is not a person who is not providing a consciousness about something. It may be an absence of the consciousness of the thing they want but it is a consciousness of the thing they get.

And so, the only way to make a demonstration is to destroy in your consciousness everything that in any objective shape or manner supposes that that thing cannot be done. Before you can do that, you have got to stop looking for the thing you do not want. If you want to be well, don't look for sickness.

People often say to me, "I have such and such, do you want to see it? It is on my arm, or on my leg. Do you want to see my foot?" What you see you image, and what you image you get. I don't want to see anybody's foot. We cannot be too careful about these things. There is a law operating.

Everything in the physical universe is manifestation of mind into what we call matter. There is a certain rate of what we call vibration. Vibration really means motion. Vibration and form, which is vibration, do not make themselves. They are not their own cause. They are the children; the father is the intelligence which sets it in motion. But nevertheless on the physical plane everything is a certain rate of vibration and everything has an attraction for itself, for anything like itself. And so on the physical plane like attracts like, and like produces like. We have heard that in the old familiar saying "Birds of a feather flock together," and, "You can tell a person by the company he keeps." So, if we have within our consciousness a certain unity with a certain thing, we are bound to attract that thing to us in the physical plane. If you and I go out and picture poverty and misery everywhere, that is what we will get. There are very few people who have overcome the fear of lack. It is nothing but fear, because if you were going to really lack you would lack anyway whether you were afraid or not. And if you and I saw these things in anybody or in affairs, we would be making mental pictures of these things.

We have not completely emancipated ourselves, but we are always struggling to get a greater realization. We must stop seeing what we do not want. There is no use in it.

Somebody was telling me of a little New Thought child, who had a manifestation of a cold and some boy said, "Oh, you have a cold." She said, "Don't you say cold to me." That little child showed a great deal more sense than the most intellectual giant in this world if he did not understand the law of cause and effect. Her childish mind knew that if she said it, it would be. How careless we are. How often do we image things we do not want? If we never said anything but what we wanted, it would come to us so fast it would almost smother us. I know that those days my consciousness is the freest and clearest and the most sure and spontaneous, those are the days that the most flows to me, the greatest opportunities, largest amounts of money—not because there are any different kinds of days, but because those days everything flows in and out with perfect freedom. I no longer try to compel anything. I have come to understand within my own consciousness a reason for everything that happens to me, or ever will. And I do not blame people or conditions anymore, or blame myself, for this is a matter of consciousness; instead, I try to provide a greater consciousness. If I want to attract a certain thing to me, if I want to attract a certain explanation of something I do not understand and that thing is written in a book, or some person knows it, I speak right out, "I want that thing," and it will come to me. I know it will. I realize within my consciousness that it is mine to have. Maybe a day or two days or a week or a month will go by, but someday it will come along. Perhaps somebody will ask me if I have read a certain book. I will say, "I never read that book," but I will take it and look into it, and I will probably find in the book the thing I wanted. Or someone will introduce someone to me who knows the thing I am seeking. About a month ago I desired to do a certain thing and I could not see the way clearly, and at last I said, "It knows what I myself want, I know just exactly what it is, something in me corresponds to it, and that something is the thing," and let it alone. And yesterday the desired information came, everything in the most wonderful way without any effort. Now, if I had said, "I cannot get that thing," I would not have provided within myself the something that knew the thing before the thing was. If you want a thing, you have got to have it in consciousness before you get it. Jesus said, "Believe when ye pray, etc." The world has read it a million times and never realized what it meant. Because everything is made out of thought in this universe. That is the only reason. No mysterious reason, no jealous God that compels you to believe in Him. Everything is made out of thought, and when you have got that you have got the thing.

Now, to align ourselves with these great realities of being, with the great activities of life, metaphysicians should not be stupid, dead kind of people, but of all the people on earth they should be interested in business, in commerce, in industry, in education, in religion, in politics, in everything that is a broad activity of the world, because they are the people who have the big concepts. Don't withdraw from things but enter into a greater consciousness, of an expanded activity with everything. You don't have to retreat to some convent with a holier-than-thou feeling. Look out—you might die. You should be so full of the essence of vitality of life you would feel as if you would explode if you did not do something. That would not make you chaotic. Be calm and peaceful, but that great sense of the activity of life, that one thing will heal you of most anything because it will just set things going and purify everything inside. Be a center of activity instead of sitting down and weeping and moaning. Your every thought will attract to you such life that you cannot be sick; it will attract to you such activity, you cannot be poor. You see that activity of life flows through everything. It would not hurt, if you wanted to demonstrate supply, for you to visualize money flowing into you until you could not get out of the way of it. You would be dealing with an actual scientific law. That is the foundation of every physical manifestation in the universe. You would not be hypnotizing yourself; you would be using an eternal and absolute principle of being. Only people who do not understand these things would think you were hypnotizing yourself.

If you would feel that you could fling your consciousness out into an infinite expansion and draw back to you everything that you want, things would circulate around more and more.

People often ask me, "What method do you use for demonstration?" I give but one answer. I know of no method except the Word. The Word is what everything comes from, the power behind everything, and that is all there is. And then the Word becomes flesh. You do not have to have any method but have to use that word in an expanded consciousness. Let it reach out and bring in more and more. The great trouble with the world is this: The world is not impersonal. There is a belief in people that they have got to suffer. But for you and me who are learning more and more of the impersonal truth, we have let go of that race belief. The ordinary people cannot be judge of anything except as to how it affects them. "How will it affect me?" It does not matter how it affects you. If you could only forget this, get this out of the way as a hindrance to your progress. If we could only throw ourselves away. What difference does it make whether you are rich or poor, or starve to death? How will it affect me? It is that clinging on in fear. If the thought that is behind all poverty would not care whether you starved to death and would say, "I could not do any more than starve, I certainly will not be afraid of it," that would loosen things up and all would be manifested. Their fears they gather to them still closer and harder until as Job said, "The thing I feared has come upon me." It is the law of attraction and you are bound by it.

We are altogether too personal in our likes and dislikes, in our picayunish ways picking and pecking like some old hen. If you are going to be a metaphysician, you cannot peck. You are now supposed to fly. But if our thoughts are limited, we are more and more beating around a bush. We have got to extend our consciousness into the universal, and realize that all there is is made for us. There is no limit to be placed upon it.

Then, if we want particular things we must unify with them, we must make our at-one-ment with them. To make our at-one-ment with health would be to attract health. You cannot make your at-one-ment with health as long as you are at-one with disease. You must shove disease away from your mind. It is not yours. It is only the personal you that thinks these things belong to you. We use a thought only as long as we want to and let go of it when we are through with it, the impersonal individual. The impersonal individual will not have a thing in his life outside of the principle that he would not just as soon let go of. It is the only way that we could complete the circle of being. The ordinary person who hangs so closely to a dime could not see a silver dollar rolling around in front of them. The big person is doing big things and is not thinking of five-cent bags of peanuts if his dream is going to build railroads. If a shipbuilder is going to build ships, that person cannot be thinking of building toys. It is the person with the big activity in business you go to when you want a big thing done. You would not take a person whose only ability was to do a little carpenter work about the house and ask that person to promote a big enterprise. The people would not be attracted. Always you will draw to you in business the people who are just like you. If your mind is small and poor, you will be in business in a poor location and once in a while somebody will come in and make a small purchase. But if your consciousness is loosened up and broadened, people will come—people who do not ask the price; they pay what the price is, because like attracts like. And so we have to provide the bigger consciousness to get the bigger thing. We must get over these little personal ideas and let our consciousness realize it is one with the infinite, it is one with all, with all opportunity, with everything.

The person who wants a concept of perfect health, real livingness, must see perfect life everywhere. What we see we think, what we think we image, what we image becomes, and so we must see perfect life everywhere in everybody. When Jesus asked the man who had palsy to stretch forth his arm, Jesus did not see a sick arm; he saw a perfect arm. Immediately it became manifest. We must see within ourselves, not a downtrodden, sick, miserable thing, and sit and pity ourselves or this we will be manifest. You are the most glorious thing God ever made—a little lower than the angels, crowned with glory and honor, manifestation of all that there is, in you, all intelligence, all activity, all life. How we belittle ourselves, how we starve our own natures. We do not dare to peep lest somebody say we blaspheme. Now, let us say what we think disregarding what other people think of it. What difference does it make what the world has thought? You are a servant of what you obey. We bring every calamity upon ourselves. That is listening to the voice of the servant. Let us emancipate ourselves once and for all. We do not care very much about the opinion of the world. It is all good and the world is good, but we are doing a new thing in a new way. We cannot do a new thing in an old way. I know of no way to be healed through affirming you are sick; I know of no method that will draw to you plenty while you affirm you are poor. That would be a house divided against itself. I do not see how it can stand. You must be one thing or the other.

Life is and we have got to take it. Good is. The evil we choose and create from false thinking. You and I naturally want to attract to us that which is good and beautiful, that which is filled with peace, power, and prosperity, and that which is spiritual and eternal. We want to express a big idea of God in our life.

Suppose then you want to attract friends. Who is there who does not want friends? First of all you are not fit to have friends until you can live without them. This is an absolute fact. The reason is this: If you are not strong enough to live alone and can only live by the aid of a friend, you are living on his life and not on your own. So first, you must stand alone, yet not alone; the Infinite stands behind everything. But you see what I mean? Having demonstrated that you can stand alone and not be lonesome, then you are fit for somebody to love you. And having become this, the universal friend, the friend of all, you cannot help attracting to you all the friendships you want. You cannot help it. Having become the universal lover, that is, the embodiment of the being of love, people are compelled to love you. You must attract to you all the love there is because you have learned what love is.

To overcome weakness, be strong. Just be strong; that is all. Don't try to overcome weakness, but forget weakness. Immediately become strong. Become strong in your own strength, because behind and within you is the strength of the Infinite. Become so strong that you would know that if everything else disappeared, you would still exist as an absolute being. That is a law; that is a premise founded upon faith. There is nothing but an increased state of being, ever unfolding our own consciousness, where more and more the I beholds the soul as it is.

Each in his separate star,
Paints the thing as he sees it
For the God of things as they are.

So, become strong, and you will gather around you strong reliable people. If your life now is little in its activity, enlarge it in your mind. Fling out your consciousness into conscious union with the big things, big activities of the human race, beyond all cosmic activities, and you will find that one by one big things will slip into your life: big opportunities to express yourself, great big things, instead of the little and limited going around and around in the same circle. You cannot do that in a personal way. You cannot do that so long as you are afraid that somebody is going to get something away from you. That attitude that thinks the universe has just enough for me and if I do not get what I want away from somebody else I won't have anything, is the very worst form of limitation. There is plenty for all, and you are just reaching out and taking what is yours.

A word of counsel to people who are seeking to demonstrate about great big things—shut up about it. Don't talk. The world does not believe, and they reflect their doubt. Keep your power within yourself. Insulate yourself, encompass yourself with it, protect yourself with it, surround yourself with it. That is putting on the armor of faith against the false thought of the human race. God can only do for you what you let God do through you. Get that great big consciousness if you want to do something that takes a great deal of money to do it, and takes a lot of understanding, a lot of people engaged in it, something that was an awful big thing. That is the point: Do something new. What if it had never been done before? That has nothing to do with it. So long as you reason that way you will attract little ideas, enough to pay your rent and suffer for righteousness' sake. There is no such thing as righteous suffering. All suffering is hellish. All suffering is false. It was never intended. If you think it is wrong not to have more than enough, you are mistaken. Do you know there is not a tree that blossoms and has leaves but what it has many, many times more than it needs. It does not need them all to furnish shade. Think of all the fish eggs. Think of the grains of sand. Nature is not only abundant and lavish but from your concept and mine it is perfectly wasteful, providing ten thousand times more than it can use. Can't we put ourselves in that care? Think of the grains of sand, the drops of water, the planets, a billion suns, each with its planetary system. Think what a billion suns means! That is the way one makes things. And do we not limit ourselves probably to the front dooryard and the back steep and four square walls? Let us get out of that little picayunish way of thinking.

Then you do not have to wonder about activity. That is it, and then you stand there in the midst of all that there is and feel yourself to be a center of the irresistible power and impulse of that love and urge. For love is more than a sentiment; nobody can withstand it. That thing which is the cause of all creation, of everything, and as you let that love flow through you, love cannot help but be attracted to you. Practically all love is personal; if you do not love me, I cannot be happy. That is all "tommyrot." If you cannot be happy because some particular person does not love you, you cannot be happy. That is truth.

Most people who think they are in love are just attracted physically. When people who are attracted on a physical plane are married and the fire and passion is burned out, there is nothing in common but a common, ordinary physical attraction and when that is gone the love is gone with it. What we need to realize is that love personifies itself. I would not discourage it. Let us do more than feel in love with that one person; it is all right, but feel everyone. Probably one at a time is better. Let us feel in love with the world. Why not extend our consciousness? Let it reach from the few and particular ones we love because we are attracted to them, that is all right, but let it go away out and beyond and over them to everybody. You cannot love until you do that, and you cannot do that while you limit love to a personal thing, and you cannot do that while you see anything unlovely in anybody. The person who presents herself to me as most unlikable, I try to see in her nothing that is unlovely. I met a lady who did not like me very well. She was spitting and sputtering one day, and I said to her, "I wonder if I look as funny to you as you do to me?" and she said, "Yes, you do, just the same." When we realize that we have not very much to say against anybody, we will realize life is universal; it is infinite. And that is what Jesus said: "When you love those that love you, or give to those that give to you, when you give from the standpoint of such a feeling, and until the time comes that in a certain sense you love your neighbor's children as your own you do not love." You do not see in them divine nature; you cannot see your own divine nature. It is absolutely impossible for you to see two different things at the same time. If you see a brat in your neighbor's child, you cannot see anything else in your own; you will see a brat. And this is why when the people brought the woman taken in adultery to Jesus, he never questioned what they said, but said to them that if they were so perfect, just take her out and stone her. That is all right, a very mean hard miserable world feels that way when it is in their own consciousness. And so do you and I. We do the same thing when we criticize anybody. You and I could not criticize unless the criticism was in us. You will see nothing in anybody else unless you have it in you to see it. You are what you say, and what you say is what you must become. You cannot see a thing in me but what you see in yourself first.

And so as we more and more create in our thought that which is perfect, that which is imperfect not only disappears but it no longer exists. It is remembered no more against us forever.

We must take our life, our love, our thought of happiness, our thought of friendship and make it all become universal. You stand manifested a friend to every living soul, in love with life, surrounded by a boundless, limitless infinite activity whose sole impulse is the dynamic power of irresistible love backed up by an Infinite Life, and Omnipotent Power. Nothing can limit it, and you stand in the midst of it. The whole universe is flooded with such life and intelligence, and it is all manifested by perfect peace. It is all yours. Reach out, or right within, and it is all yours.

It is bubbles we buy with a whole soul's tasking;
'Tis heaven alone that is given away,
'Tis only God may be had for the asking.

Business Affairs
from the Standpoint
of Mental Cause

It is not difficult for ordinary people, whether or not they have any understanding of metaphysics, to believe that their thought has a great deal to do with their body. Practically everybody today can readily see that their thought largely governs their body.

It is the accepted teaching of psychology, which has become one of the principal parts of modern thought, so that we seldom find anybody who doubts the power of the mind, or thought, over the body. They may not all believe quite as far as we do. Yet I find many people who say, "Why, yes, I believe thought has a great deal to do with the body, but I do not believe it could heal such and such a thing." Well, of course, if you admit that your thought has anything at all to do with your body physically, you have to admit, although you may not have thought it out and said that you admit it, you have, from the standpoint of logical reasoning that your thought governs the processes of your body. Either your thought has everything to do with it or it has nothing at all to do with it. But these same people, many of them who even believe that

thought absolutely controls the body, find it is a little more difficult for them to say that thought can control their conditions. But
if there is anything that the new way of thinking is teaching and
demonstrating it is that our thought can absolutely control our
health, our environment, our business. The reason why people do
not understand this is because they have not realized what Mind is.
Ordinary people think of mind only from the limitation of their
own environment, and the concept they have of mind is the concept they have of their own way of thinking, which is, indeed, very
limited, and if our possibility of demonstrating the metaphysical
principle depended upon our limited understanding, it would be
very slight, but it does not.

We are surrounded by an All-Seeing-Knowing Mind, and that
is the mind we talk about in metaphysics. We are not talking about
your mind and my mind. This is where the error comes in. Figure
that if you have a mind and I have a mind and somebody else has
a mind and realize there could not any of us manifest mind unless
there was a Mind from which thought could draw the intelligence
that we are. And think of the universe then as being permeated
simply by Mind, not by minds many. The belief in dual mind has
sapped and destroyed practically all philosophies and all religions
of all ages and will continue to do it until the world philosophi-
cally and religiously arrives at the conclusion that there is but One.
Whatever they may call that One, there is but One. So, instead of
saying that you have a mind and I have a mind, let us say *Mind is,*
and every living soul is in it and uses that Mind which is.

Now, that Mind which is, is creative and it is creation. We
think into it and it takes that thought and does the thing. You have
no responsibility once you have thought. You do not have to wonder whether or not there is something going to do it. It will be
done all right if you are constant in your thinking. So, consider

that here is a mind; I want you to see that your business is absolutely controlled by your thought, absolutely. Here is a Mind and you are in it and your business is in it. Now, this Mind is going to operate through your thought about the things that you deal with. Now, your thought, then, operating in Mind produces your business. I do not want you to think of your thought doing it directly as a thing outside of Mind, but your thought operative through this one principle produces your affair. Your mind is the thinker, and *the Mind does it.*

Now, of course, since there is but one Mind, whatever mind you have or I have that we call our mind is simply manifestation of the One; so that you, or I, all that we are, are centers in this Mind or thought activity. There is not a thing that appears in the manifest universe but what it is an objectified thought, whether it is a bump on your head or a corn on your foot, or a mountain or a planet. It could not be there if it was not made out of Mind. You only get something where there is something to get it out of.

Your mind absolutely controls your individual world, your thought through the power of the Infinite Principle of Mind. Whether or not that Infinite Mind is God, I am not here to discuss. To me it simply means that it is like electricity. It is a power which is, and that Mind has to have a center in us in order to create. Consequently, I think of God as the living intelligence which is the reason for mind and electricity, and peanuts and planets and people and everything else and so thought, intelligence, and mind is our manifestation of as much intelligence as we have, which is as much as we understand of God, no more and no less. Our ability and mind to know depend upon our ability to know God.

When it comes to using Mind, we are not manipulating God; we are just using natural law. There is nothing sacrilegious about it; it is not blasphemous. There is a mental principle that you can use.

Mind *is* and it flows through everything. A wise and intelligent person would realize that it has to be and then would get busy and begin to use it. And that is what people ought to do. Our understanding of God, our spiritual thinking, gives us a higher power from the mental standpoint, but we are still governed by the law we set in motion. So, let each of us think about God as we choose; that is not anybody else's business, but when it comes to using the creative principle of mind, you have got to use it in a certain way or you cannot get results—not because of any arbitrary thing, not because of any jealous God. And if there is a God, that God does not know there is such a thing as jealousy. God knows that we are, and that we are all right. God does not know about anything unlike itself. And so you and I have got to emancipate ourselves from these little picayunish ideas of the universe, and know that God, Spirit, is Infinite Love and Intelligence, Wisdom and Power, and that is enough.

You and I may worship this God as we see fit. Your manner of approaching the Deity may be entirely different from mine and might be the best way. You might get a greater sense of the touch of the Divine Hand if you went to a certain place and worshiped in a certain way. If you say it is good, that is good. Somebody else might do it by going fishing, etc. It is good. There are no churches and church times in the universal God; there is just simply *I am*, and there is not anything else. And so let every living soul forget what individuals do and how they attempt to reach God, and mind their own affairs, just reach God within themselves.

But when it comes to using the law, you are not praying to God. When it comes to using the law, you have got to understand the law you are using and use it in a scientific, definite way to get results. Edison does not pray to God to reveal electricity to him, yet, in a certain sense he does. He makes his mind receptive to something that comes out of the atmosphere; that is, intelligence, one with the inspiration of the Spirit. But when he gets it he takes it and scientifically applies it to the known principle. There is no chaotic thinking about it.

If you and I want to apply definitely the realization of Mind, we realize that Mind governs everything and that we are living in a mental universe and that as far as you and I are concerned depends upon what we think, and what we think must depend on what we believe. When you say that you do not believe all is Mind, you do not believe there is any such thing as that, you could not get any result. I have had people say to me, "I tried it, but it didn't work; I knew it wouldn't." Don't you see? They have mentally denied the thing they are seeking to make; and if all is Mind and they do this, they neutralize their thought and zero is the result. We have got to believe it is and for those who believe it is, it will work. With those who do not, it is nobody's fault. Do not pick and choose; everybody is alike. The person the world calls the best is not one iota better than the person they call the worst. It is only our different way, and their different way, of looking at things.

Believing that Mind is, you have got a principle which is absolute. It is exact. It is going to correspond to your thinking about it. So the first great necessity is to believe it; without that, you could not do anything. That is why Jesus said, "It is done unto you as you believe." Always it is done unto people as they believe, and there is something that does it.

We must believe that our work is acted upon and around by this Mind. For instance, you want to demonstrate activity in your business. You believe that word is the Divine law about that thing. There is something that takes it up and executes it for you; then, if you have accepted the thought that all is Mind and that thought is the thing, you will see right off that your word is the power behind the thought, and it depends upon the word or the thought that you are forming. And so plastic is Mind, so receptive, that the very slightest thought makes an impression in it; you cannot help that. Most everybody is thinking so many kinds of thoughts, which pass each other and lack harmony. It is no wonder they are getting such results in their lives. If a gardener plants a thousand kinds of seeds, he has a thousand kinds of plants. You plant the seed of thought.

You know that your word goes forth as absolute law, that it is acted upon by this Mind and executed. Since that is true, everything depends upon our mental concept, thought; "As a man thinketh in his heart so is he." The Bible reiterates that statement and expresses a thousand times the creative power of thought. That is all there was to the teaching of Jesus. He said, "I am just doing what you can do, it is through the power." The centurion, coming to Jesus, recognized the power of the word which the man speaks, for he said, "I also am one in authority." He was clever to recognize another man who was in authority. He said, "I have this authority on this physical plane, and I recognize that you are a man who acts with authority on an invisible plane. All you have to do is to speak the word." And so he spoke the word and something responded. Speak the word only and it shall be done. Again, the Bible tells us that the word is in our own mouth and it is not afar off. Not lo here nor lo there; it is within us. That place is within you and within me. The responsibility of our own life is ours. Every living soul is going to wake up to the fact that everybody is a different individuality and that they have absolute control over their life and that beyond that an Infinite Intelligence watches over it and sees that nothing happens by chance. Then they will have a broader concept of God, a greater tolerance for their neighbor and a greater realization of their divine nature.

You and I are beginning to see this, but we are not getting the results we should. If you have on the one hand an infinite principle which could make anything, which is a law which we have and prove right here, and on the other hand our own God-given power to use it, why do we not draw forth more? It is merely because we do not provide a greater concept. You hold an image up, you hold an object in front of a mirror and it will image in the mirror the exact size of the object. You hold a thought in mind and it will image back into matter the exact likeness of the thought. You take this image that you hold in front of the mirror and change it ever so slightly and there will be a change in the mirror. It is just the same in the mental.

There are very few people who can hold a definite thought, I do not mean hold a thought. I mean get a clear grasp of things, a good mental picture. Most of us fluctuate every time we see anything in the external. If our friend gets sick, it would discourage us and then we would get all jumbled up. This is why many of us are just twiddling along. It has nothing to do with the greatness of re-alization of what is infinite. The person who has accepted this will never doubt. If you believe that God is the only power there is, and you know, as you believe God is the only power there is you will never believe in a devil. There is nothing that can oppose Almighty God. The human race has tried to make a pagan God. There is no God of war; there is only a God of peace. Righteousness is in the war we are in, but that does not create a God of war. If we are right, right is on our side. We know we are right. If God is a God of war, he is on one side as well as on the other. Evil comes in darkness to destroy, means simply the absence of God, or the ab-sence of recognition of our conception of God.

The human race has tried to make God as a king. It is not un-usual to see a picture of God, even in our day and generation. I have seen a picture of God in a newspaper; God is turning over the pages of a book and reading the history of the human race. When you think there are one thousand million suns and God only knows how many planets, God could not be just a man reading a book. We have got to get over these little concepts and begin to provide a bigger realization of the universal. We must not deny that which we affirm. If there is a power that can hold everything in its place in the universe, that power is enough and we do not have to look to any human aid for anything or anybody. You and I reason only from cause which is spiritual and mental, and we begin to use this light, so what we have got to do is to weed out from our thought everything that denies it. There is something in the race consciousness that says we are poor, we are limited, there is a lack of opportunity, times are hard, prices are high, nobody wants to spend money, et cetera. They are all of them a mistake and have got to go. Never a person succeeded who thought that way. We are using a destructive power, but we do not know it. Every thought like that must go and every individual must realize that he or she is an active center of the Lord God Almighty. Enjoy that supreme intelligence from the Absolute. We are given dominion over everything. We must speak forth what we believe and not what we do not want. It was Paul, I believe, that said, "Why is it that that which I would do I do not and that which I would not do I do?" But I do not know any reason why we should not be better than Paul. I think we should do better than he did.

Jesus told the people, "I have got to go because you depend upon me. You think I am doing it. It is expedient that I go but the Spirit of Truth will come then to you and awaken you to your own consciousness and then you will know what I am talking about." As long as we are depending upon anything or anyone, even upon Jesus Christ, we are depending upon something that is outside.

That does not take anything from Jesus Christ; he is still all and more than we thought he was, but we must awaken and realize that the divine consciousness is within us. This is the mystery that has been hid from the foundation of the world, Christ Jesus in you.

The individual must awaken to the consciousness, that within, God has placed the living word which is still the word of God operating through us. God everywhere, God in you and me speaking the word and the word becomes me. So you must believe that it is within you. So, what would you do, sitting within the midst of your affairs? You would say, "I am activity, God is activity, God through me is creative, the power of my word creates activity. And the funny part of it all is that anybody that says that and believes it, acts. And if every other living soul on the face of the earth would say it was a lie, it would work just the same for the person who believed. There was a time when different individuals thought the world was flat, but that did not make it flat, and I have never heard that they flattened it out in any particular place. So it is just our way of thinking about reality, and therefore admits that which is real to appear. We have not got to take upon our shoulders, from the infinite sense, any sense of responsibility. We have only to provide the thought and the power of our word carries it into effect. We should realize that the word which I speak unto you, it is Spirit and does live. In other words, your word will fulfill itself. And Jesus had such complete confidence in his word that he said, "Heaven and earth shall pass away, et cetera." We have always thought that because Jesus said that, it was because Jesus was God and could do as he saw fit. Jesus said it because he knew the law. So, you and I can say the same thing, and we must say it. The word which we speak shall fulfill itself. If it is something you need, it will come out and bring it to you. If it is something that you want and you do not know the way, it, the law, will find the way. If you want intelligence, it will provide it; for there is somebody or something that will bring it to you. All you have to do is to make known your desire, with joy and expectancy. How little trust we have. Our ordinary praying is beseeching an unkind and unwilling God to do something for Jesus' sake. We are men and women and we must look at things as they are. The world has made a mistake. Somewhere something has been wrong. If it was wrong with God, the earth would be destroyed. It is only people that are wrong; God is all right. We have been wrong and it is time we were waking up to the fact and find out what is wrong.

As knowledgeable as we are this moment, you and I, if we were to utter a prayer right now, wouldn't we be tremendously surprised if it appeared right out of the air. And yet, Jesus took five thousand people into the desert and manifested bread and fishes with which to feed them. How surprised we would be. We would be surprised if our prayer was answered at all. The ordinary person who prays has no more expectancy of that prayer being answered or it would be answered, or there is no such thing as fulfillment of faith.

Prayer is nothing but a mental attitude. Prayer is nothing you eat, nothing you smell, nothing you taste, nothing you feel, but you cannot pray without thinking. Every word is an audible expression of a thought, and therefore, the ultimate essence of prayer is your thought. We do not care how high that prayer may be; it is simply a higher way of thinking, that is all. It is nothing but a simple and direct, positive believing, a mental attitude. That is all that prayer is. So if you and I could make ourselves mechanically believe, that would be praying with faith. It is the complete faith in God and God's law. Therefore, it is the most spiritual philosophy the world has ever known. It is absolute reliance upon God. So careful is a metaphysician to rely upon God that one does not care about people at all. All human beings are liars; God is truth. They cease to believe in what their brain says. Even that thing is false because it is a thing we made through the false power of our thought, and God can do a better thing for us. And only that person whose consciousness is high spiritually can expect to get the greatest results. Jesus said, "Don't follow me for the loaves and fishes." "Seek ye the kingdom of heaven, and all these things shall be added unto you."

And so, we have come to the law as a little child, absolutely believing. We believe in the goodness of everything, in the loveliness of all things, in the ultimate power of righteousness through all things, in the power of the word, steadfastly using it, absolutely denying everything else even though it appears as a seeming reality in our life. Keep right on denying the false appearances and they will go; keep on affirming the truth and it will appear. There is a law behind everything, and using the spiritual power of your thought in the greatest confidence, believing this thought, and you do not have to go any further. Behind it all is the Omnipotent Power, the power of the Lord God Almighty. If it is in your business, speak it right there; it is good, everywhere. Get the perfect vision, the perfect concept. Enlarge your consciousness until it realizes all good and then swing right off and use this Almighty Mind. And feel daily a greater and greater sense of that communion with the Universal Spirit, God within you, God of Everywhere. And just know when you have spoken that word the law will do the rest for you. You have sowed the seed into the universal mind of the Absolute and so you can rest in peace. You can make known your requests with thanksgiving, and thus we trust in the Lord. Do not make haste because it shall be done through all living souls as they believe.

There Is So Much More

When people begin to realize that we are living in a mental universe, or a spiritual universe, they have to rethink all of their philosophy. They no longer can give a physical reason or meaning to life because there is no physical reason or meaning in life at all. So the premise of all thinkers of all ages has invariably been that all is Mind. Since all is Mind, we have to explain life from that premise if we explain it correctly.

Since all is Mind and the activity of Mind is thought, thought is law. Law being an activity of Mind, which Mind is infinite and one, consequently becomes absolute. In the life of the individual, then, we have this Mind which we use. It is the principle of life. Into it we think; back from it we draw manifestation of our thought. So, if you and I want to give a reason for riches or poverty, we could not give a physical reason, because there isn't any.

We could not give a spiritual reason, if by spirit we mean God, because God is so much more. Not even a tree is created but what it bears many times more leaves than is necessary. There is so much more of everything in the physical universe than the human race ever has need of or ever could, and there is so much more wasted than they ever had or ever could that we cannot attribute limitation to God or to causation; because out of that cause itself is made things in such abundance that it would be impossible to use even the smallest fraction of them. Since we can no longer blame God and since there is nothing but God and ourselves that we have to deal with, there is no longer any question but what we must blame ourselves for whatever is wrong. No, we do not have to blame ourselves maliciously and censure ourselves maliciously. The sensible person will realize that whatever has been done that is wrong has been done, not because of sin, maliciously, but because of ignorance, unintentionally. I do not want to be poor and sick and unhappy, and I give you credit for having as much brains as I. I do not know of anybody who really wants to be sick, poor, or unhappy, and yet a large portion of the human race are, and it is their own fault; not necessarily their individual sin, but it is their fault through a lack of the recognition of truth. Ignorance of the law excuses no one, so we come under the ignorant use of the law.

Since all is Mind and Mind returns to the thinker of thought objectified, what we think, what we hold within ourselves as a mental attitude, becomes the mental equivalent of creative spirit or causation, and the objective life or external result, our environment in the without. Our way of thinking and believing then is the sole medium between causation and its flow through us into manifestation of our affairs. We believe that medium is our thought processes, conscious and unconscious.

There are two ways whereby the individual builds up a subjective consciousness. Your subjective consciousness is not a mind separated from you; it is not another mind in you. Subjective consciousness is simply the attraction of thought in the past gathered around you. It is your power of attraction. You can see how that would be. Since there is but one, that which we call subjective mind, which is a reality, and what we are depends largely upon the subjective state of our thinking. Instead of saying objective mind, we should say subjective state of thought. These thoughts which we have created in the past and which still are around us, and the thoughts which we have and still are attracting, this is the medium which we build between Spirit and matter. So what we are and what we shall become depends absolutely upon the state of our subjective thought because that is the power or process within us.

There are two ways by which this subjective thinking is created. One is through race suggestion and the other is through personal suggestion or auto-suggestion. Under the heading of race suggestion would come prenatal conditions and influences, heredity, environment, and what the human race has always believed. Since all is Mind and your life and mine are but an activity of Mind or thinking forth process, or a state of consciousness, which consciousness when it comes with clear thinking—and we cannot hinder its coming because everything is mental activity—it is a matter of course from that. What people have always thought has done the same thing, and the world is filled with that form of thought influence, that psychic influence. Ordinary psychics, not understanding what they are doing, being those who see thought and the form it takes, though generally ignorant of what they are doing, seeing these forms of thought, think they are seeing realities. They are seeing nothing but visions, they are really nothing. People have created an activity in Mind. Thought can come forth in Mind, which Mind is in a perfect equilibrium where there is no friction, and unless it is stopped by an opposite thought it will exist forever, as far as we know. And so each one of us is immersed in a race belief which fills our consciousness with false thought which claims to be true. That is one way of limitation.

The other is impressed upon us by auto-suggestion as we view things in the outside. As we look at things so we think, but as we think, as we mentally image, so we become.

Before people can realize the truth which is to free them from conditions, they have to eliminate all thought that is negative as a race suggestion and as an auto-suggestion. From the standpoint of the race suggestion, they must erase from their mentality any beliefs within that they are born with a limited condition. They must realize in its place that they have a spiritual birth, born from an infinite source, that they are now living in it and filled with limitless life and boundless freedom. You can go further than that and, realizing the power of your word, declare that it destroys within you any thought of limitation. You must go still further than that and cease suggesting to your own self unconsciously any auto-suggestion that you are limited. That means to cease to rely upon or believe in or talk about or dwell upon or listen to anybody who talks limitation. I know of no way, since all is Mind, whereby an individual can do one thing and believe another. There is not any way. And so we find ordinary individuals are neutralizing their efforts as fast as they are thinking. Thinking correctly for fifteen or twenty minutes and thinking negatively for the next fifteen or twenty minutes neutralizes it, and so they find themselves in a constant state of chaos and confusion. It is not an easy matter to free ourselves from race consciousness. I do not imagine that anybody has completely done it. Jesus himself didn't do it because he transcended every human law, so-called, and I imagine that in as far as we learn to transcend in our thought that law which the human race has set up, that we will do the same thing.

If you want to eliminate thoughts of limitation, you must recognize that they have to be eliminated only about yourself. There is a universal principle that does the rest. You are in that Mind just like a point in a circle. You are constantly thinking out into it. It is the principle of all life. If that were not true, there could not be a manifestation of the world as we see it. It would be absolutely impossible. It is the only explanation that can be given, and because it is the only explanation that can be given the wise people of all ages from Moses down to Plato and Socrates, and philosophers and teachers of all ages, have come to the same conclusion and have realized from time immemorial its absolute truth. People in widely separated sections of earth have reached the same conclusions, which is a further proof of the impersonality of the law. Where an individual contact is, there it is. And so the same truth has been revealed to thousands of different people in different ages and different classes, who spoke different languages, but the same truth has been interpreted by them through their mouths, or thinking. The Oriental would naturally have a mystic way of doing it, and different people would do it each in their own way. We would do it more clearly than any other class of people on earth for the reason that American people think more rapidly, more clearly, quicker. They see quicker than any other nation that has ever lived. But it would be nevertheless the same thing. God did not come down from the top of the mountain and say to Moses, "I have something to tell you confidentially." Moses went up into the mountain and thought, "Like produces like," and he came to the same conclusion. With the law of Moses, there is the foundation of our law today. It was a purely impersonal thing with Moses. That stands for the impersonal—law—exacting justice from the personal. It is nothing but a law of cause and effect. "An eye for an eye and a tooth for a tooth." That is simply a statement of the fact that the law returns to us what we give to it. Nothing else, cause and effect. As I think into the law, the law gives back to me. Jesus did not destroy the law of Moses. He said, "I come not to destroy but to fulfill." Moses prophesied that a greater one than he should come. The law would still be as exacting as it had been under Moses' interpretation because it was universal. The name revealed the love which is the impulse of all creation. He did not say, "You are no longer subject to law," but, "This is the law and the prophets," and "God is love."

Jesus said the same thing when he said, "As ye think so shall it be done unto you," and "Judge not lest ye be judged for with what judgment ye judge ye shall be judged," and "With what measure ye meet it shall be measured to you again." Do you see?

And there is another thing you must not overlook. Jesus taught people "It is done unto you." Upon the impersonality of the law you must dwell. It is done unto you. We are thinkers—Mind creates. We do not create. The united intelligence of the human race since time immemorial does not make that (indicating something and saying—that is too small for you to see it, it is not anything). We are the thinkers into Mind and Mind is the principle of life that returns thought objectified unto the thinker—and therefore it is returned as I believe. If you believe in poverty, you cannot believe in riches. To find a physical proof of it, you go and see a successful person who has made money in this world. That person carries the very image of success within. And failure carried the image of failure. If you could see a person's inner consciousness and outer condition, they would merge into each other with no differentiation. One is the image and the other is the reflection as you hold it up before a mirror.

The human consciousness is full of error, and we must destroy it. How are we going to do that? It sounds logical enough, but how are you going to do it? You are going to do it by doing the right thing in the same way you did the wrong thing, only you are going to do it differently. If you could not do this, it would be impossible to do it at all. You are going to take the negative thought and convert it into positive thought. You are going to destroy the negative with the positive. There is nothing but Mind and that which it manifests in the universe. Each of us is a center in this Mind, eternally thinking into it. Because of its absolute receptivity, its unconditional power of creation and of the impulse which makes it create everything that it holds, the moment you think, something begins to form around that thought. And so the human race has bound itself by the very thing which should have freed it. The kingdom of heaven is within. The word, which is in your own mouth. *Job says, "That which, et cetera."* And Isaiah, "So shall the word be that goes forth from my mouth." That very word that was given us to use, because of our ignorance, we have misused. That ignorance, the Bible tells us, came because man (Adam) ate of the fruit of the tree of knowledge of good and evil, which means that he knew good and evil. Did he believe that a negative equaled a positive, or that nothing equaled something? Believing that and living in a world of Mind, the negative thought created the form of itself and he suffered. Now we realize that if that philosophy were true, that nothing equaled something, or a negative equaled a positive, when the two meet they would neutralize themselves and zero would be the result, and you would not have any universe at all. There is no such thing as a negative power only so long as we give it power. It could have no power over the truth. If it did, nothing would equal something, which is simply an impossibility.

Realizing that and that all is Mind and that we think—you and I—you have a ready instrument in yourself which without fear you can use to neutralize that thought. So you will take the positive thought, and what would you do? Here is a thing which few people understand in this world. I am one of those few or I would not be talking—I have to claim something. Now, there is Mind—

most everybody who goes into New Thought, Metaphysics, Psychology (there is very little difference between Metaphysics and Modern Psychology), most everybody gets confused because of a few simple things. Now, many people here have read Hudson's *Law of Psychic Phenomena*. Hold up your hands. That's good. It is a wonderful book. If only he had realized that his subjective mind is one with his conscious mind. That is the way to look at it. I have my mind here and there is your mind there, and I will suggest something to your mind. That is all wrong. There is nothing but Mind—that is all there is, and you and I are in this Mind which is all there is and as I think forth into this Mind I produce a thought vibration. We cannot think without producing a vibration in Mind any more than a fish can move in the water without stirring the water. We cannot think without stirring up Mind. This Mind is always receptive, a creative power, and it immediately begins to operate upon our thought. You and I are acted upon; that is, our bodies and our conditions are acted upon. As we think about them, Mind acts upon them. If I wanted to treat my body myself, I would sit down in a chair and I would realize the truth about this, the activity of Mind. Then I would say I am treating Ernest Holmes, and I would treat myself just as if I were treating somebody else. I would declare about Ernest Holmes. As Jesus said, "It is done unto you." Do you see the difference between that and thinking everybody has a separate mind? Then there it is, the easiest thing in the world to heal this way. If I were to treat your conditions of Mind, I would set them right out in mind and declare about them, and my responsibility ends. It is done unto everybody as they believe—believe it is done unto them by an infinite power. Everybody is their own heaven or hell. I do not believe there is any halfway position in this world. People are either happy or miserable; they are sick or they are well; they are rich or they are poor; they are in heaven or they are in hell.

To realize, first we think forth into Mind and infinite power does it unto us. That is where it takes time to stop and think, because it is a fact that the individual's consciousness grows as in some small measure, infinity is grasped. Of course we cannot grasp infinity—that is impossible—but as we grasp at it, it must forever enlarge our possibilities of thinking forth into Mind, and mind itself being infinity, it is limitless. We limit it; therefore, it seems limited to us. That limitation is nothing but a false belief. It says in the Old Testament, of the Children of Israel, they could not enter in because of their unbelief and because they limited the Holy One of Immanuel. That comes to us as race suggestion, limitation. You know we cough, because somebody else coughed. We have Spanish influenza because "they" have it. People get it where they could not have taken it by contagion, mentally contagious is disease. And we are poor because we believe in poverty. We are the only beings in the world that want and such animals as we have domesticated, they want. When nature is let alone, the rose does not run out of color, the bird does not run out of song; the water never ceases to fall or the tide to ebb and flow. There is plenty of scent in the flower, there is plenty of water in the ocean; plenty of sand on the shore, plenty. And did you ever think of the number of eggs the fish lay? If they all hatched, the fish would choke the ocean. There is nothing limited but us. Standing supreme in intelligence on the face of the earth we are more limited. A bird coming from the north builds a winter home with more ease than the millionaire in Pasadena, and far more beautiful, and flies away when it is done with it. And you and I are the only things that feel sick and miserable and unhappy and bound and poor. And do you know we are bound with our own freedom? If we were not first free, we could not be bound.

The plant is mechanical, the ocean is mechanical, the planet and the stars are mechanical, and the animals, while not limited to a certain spot, are more or less mechanical. Life flows through them with that impulse of plenty which it inherently has, and we sit and stare because at the threshold of human consciousness God has to stand and wait for recognition. "Behold: I stand at the door and knock." The self chooses. We have chosen nothing and that is why we have nothing. When we wake up and begin to desire something, we shall find it is right there. This we do. Not only is there an activity of mind and spirit ready, but it is surging forward with tremendous power. The seed that grows in the crevice in the wall has power to burst the wall. That is why Jesus said, "The Father seeketh." That is the great lesson we learn from the story of the prodigal son. He chose, he went out from the house of his father. Nobody said he could not go. He lived with the pigs and nobody said he was not made to live with the pigs. Nobody said a word. But as long as he stayed in the pigpen, there he was. He had a perfect right to live with the pigs if he wanted to. But when he began to wake up and say to himself "Home was never like this," and he started back home, he had only got halfway when the father came out to meet him. That is the greatest truth in spiritual history. That is, Causation comes out to meet the individual halfway, the individual who turns toward it. We have chosen nothing and Mind has created for us what we have chosen, materialized the thought, and so have made a false form of thought. If you can erase that thought, it will go. I was once treating, I think I have told you this a good many times. (*Gives illustration of the cancer which disappeared and returned again several times before healed.*) Where did it come from and where did it go? It came and went, it did, the whole thing, through some operation of thought. There is not any question about it. Finally it went and stayed away. There was fluctuation of the thought image behind it, the thought came and went, and the thing came and went with it.

So thought has created individuals, and we are just beginning to wake up to our divine individuality. And we find that the very thing which was placed in us and made our divine individualities and gave us power, limited us. We are bound by our own freedom. We awake and find ourselves in possession of an infinite power on the one hand to use, but a limited concept to use it with. What do you need? If the concept automatically externalizes the thing, and it does, because people get sick, because they get well. They did not know that thought slipped in unawares. If we could realize that thought works unconsciously and we have not a big enough concept, we have to get a bigger concept. Get a concept that realizes it is no longer subject to the race belief, that it no longer needs to see that which it does not want to express: a concept that learns to see the perfect. Lots of people think the world is going to hell. If it is, it will all go together. They think the world is getting worse and worse. That is false. The world is getting good so fast that you and I don't have to see an imperfect world. It is true that we are in war and we support it with everything we have got because it is right, but don't you know we can go through this war and not see trouble. You and I can go up and down the street without seeing a person that is lame. I can give a dollar to a beggar and not see poverty. If all is Mind, and there is no other conclusion, if we see sick people we cannot heal it. California seems to be full of such individuals, but we must not see them. You cannot heal that which you see. Healing is unseeing that which is wrong and seeing that which is right. I have no patience with people who have not strength of character enough to be human and still be divine. If you have to go to a convent to keep from being contaminated by the world, you are not strong enough to do it any good. The place to live is right in the world and enjoying everything. We have not got to put on a long face to be good, in order to understand spiritual things. That flower is spiritual and you will find it growing by the roadside. Everything that is human is spiritual; everything that is human is divine. The only thing is that people have not understood it. So you will find that instead of getting that old sense of suffering for righteousness' sake, there is not anybody sick you have to suffer for. God does not suffer. Jesus did not suffer. Jesus went his way rejoicing. He said, "I have come that ye shall have life." That we might enjoy, might learn. We have had too much of the old tradition of Christ suffering, crucified, bloody, and miserable. Instead, we should see the glorious resurrected Christ. Jesus did not have to worry about lack or being sick or poor. That is a lie. Was that man poor who could materialize loaves and fishes for five thousand, turn water into wine, walk on the water, calm the storm, et cetera. His robe was so priceless they would not tear it to pieces. Talk about Jesus' life on earth! We have more records of him at feasts and weddings than anywhere else. And the very thing they criticized him for was that he ate with publicans and sinners and drank wine.

We do not have to do anything but get right with ourselves. Those individuals who can get right with themselves in seeing the whole situation by believing they are worthwhile and believe they are good, and believe in the infinite power they use, and declare the infinite power within them, do not have to ask anybody whether it is true.

It resolves itself into simplicity. You and I are surrounded by Mind, and that power is the only power in the universe. I do not know what it is, how it works, where it came from; I do not know anything about it, and neither does anybody else who ever lived, and possibly we never shall. I only know that it is, and we only know that it is because we get a result. And in getting a result we are justified in believing it is. Use it and benefit by it. And for every person who receives it, it will work. If it is healing, if it is making them happy, if it is attracting some better thing, it is doing that. So we are thinking into that undifferentiated substance which eternally is forming around our thought and returning it to us manifested. Jesus, realizing the divine power of his own word, said, "Heaven and earth shall pass away, but my word shall not pass away until all be fulfilled." That is the word that is in your own mouth and in Mind.

Part III

A Series of Private Lessons

Given in the 1918-1920 era
(exact dates unknown)

The Science of
the Absolute

The following is a series of twelve private class lectures that include questions from students and answers by Ernest Holmes. At this time Ernest Holmes calls his philosophy the Science of the Absolute. Please keep in mind the era of these lectures; therefore, the vocabulary and economic circumstances may be very different from contemporary standards. Some of the lectures were recorded as cryptic notes, while most were transcribed in their entirety.

Introduction

All of your work begins and ends in your consciousness because mind is all there is. In making a demonstration, you have not one iota of responsibility; it all rests with mind.

We are surrounded by a thinking stuff which permeates all the inner-spaces of the universe. It is the original; it was, is, and always shall be.

Heaven is lost for want of an idea, for lack of perception and nothing else.

Every living soul is a point of personified God-consciousness, immutable, allness, power, *now*. You are not approaching the point but you are that *now*.

Fearlessly announce that you are the truth and nothing but the truth. Know that within you now dwells the eternal God, for all the presence, all the power, and all the God there is, is with you and in you now.

Question: As the quality and quantity of demonstrations depend on your mental equivalent, how can we best enlarge it?

Ernest Holmes: You must realize that everything is mind, nothing moves but intelligence: there is nothing to move but intelligence. Take the intelligence away from the body, and the body will not get sick or well. The smartest people in the world, the most intelligent, are the ones who conduct the business of the world. The greatest artists, the ones who are the most interested along that line, are the ones who succeed. An artist has a mental equivalent of art which the businessman does not have. The big businessman could not paint a beautiful picture; however, he has a mental equivalent of a big business.

The Standard Oil Company is the most perfect commercial enterprise that has ever been evolved. The only other most perfect organization in the world is the Catholic Church. The Christian Science Church stands third. It is governed by one directing intelligence. It becomes very arbitrary in doing it, but back of it is intelligence working.

We must have a mental equivalent. We must recognize what mental equivalent means. A person who works for ten dollars a week has no mental equivalent for five hundred dollars. There must be something inside of us which equals the thing that we want to do. Water will reach its own level by its own weight. If you would equally distribute money among everybody, in two or three years, those who have no mental equivalent will not have the money. The people who are the most intelligent along these lines get it all back.

If a person is getting fifty-five dollars a week, how can he or she demonstrate one hundred dollars a week? Speak it out definitely in mind—one hundred dollars a week. Realize that there is nothing but intelligence, substance, and form. Be definite in your mind. Get the consciousness and speak it; and as your inner consciousness corresponds to the form of the external word, it will be.

Question: Is there life after death?

Ernest Holmes: I don't see how there can be life after death. There can't be any; there is no life after death because there is no death. It is just a continuation of life.

The Nature of God

The nature of God and the nature of the human are the same. One is the macrocosm and the other microcosm.

The three phases of God are:

First, intelligence, infinity, allness, totality, life principle, all that is, was, or ever will be.
Second, substance, universal, plastic, subjectivity, creative power or mind, omnipresent.
Third, form—all form which has ever existed or ever shall exist.

In the beginning God moved upon the face of the deep according to the scriptures and creation began. *Water,* esoterically speaking, means spirit. This means that God moved upon God and what was made was God; and God is all there was, and all there was, was God. There is nothing relative in the universe; there is nothing but the Absolute.

In the beginning God conceived or thought substance. God then thought upon this substance and made form. This substance was within God; for where else could God go for this substance when there was nothing but God. God thought this substance, and it was made. God thought upon Itself and produced all that is. This you must know, if you will ever demonstrate money.

Everything is of the one ultimate substance. All substance is as indestructible as God, for it is all God. God's center is everywhere and circumference is nowhere.

Humans are an identity of volition and choice in God, Infinite. There is no such thing as your mind and my mind. There is just Mind in this Infinite circle, this limitless circle without circumference.

In healing all you need is to know that you and the patient are one in God. When treating yourself or another person remember that when you speak a positive suggestion, you must be sure there is no negative suggestion given mentally from the subconscious. This is often done automatically and unconsciously, and is the result of previous suggestion or race suggestion. Such suggestions may neutralize your positive thought without you knowing anything about it. This applies to every form of manifestation: money, health, and so forth.

Intelligence, substance, and form are the root or basis of manifestation or demonstration. We know the state of our subjectivity partakes of the subjectivity of the Universe. It performs its wonderful works because it is Infinite.

Subconscious does not mean unconscious. All subjectivity is

creative, neutral, impersonal, plastic, cosmic matter, mind stuff, limitless thing. Every thought that you think is projected into it. Matter is spirit solidified and is all good. The fact that there is one substance, all of God, proves unity. The materialist sees an outside without an inside. The idealist sees the inside with no outside.

The Nature of the Human

We are one individuality though we are the three phases: body, mind and spirit.

> The first phase includes: the body, the physical, the brain, matter, objective life, manifestation, intellect, objective mind, effect, and all that did not make itself.
>
> The second phase includes: the subjective mind, subconscious, consciousness, unconsciousness, soul, creative power, feminine, plastic, neutral, impersonal, receptive, medium, absolute receptivity.
>
> The third phase includes: spirit, super-consciousness, Christ-consciousness, the real person, the image of God, complete, perfect, infinite.

The brain does not think nor cannot think. Subjective mind is amenable to suggestion. There are only two kinds of reasoning, namely: inductive and deductive. The objective mind reasons both ways. The subjective mind reasons only deductively. The subjective mind is simply law. Hypnotism proves that the subjective accepts everything that is given it. The subjective accepts both the erroneous and the true and accepts everything as the truth. Our subjectivity is a part of the omniscient mind. Before God began to create, the avenues through which to work were planned; namely, men and women, the masculine and the feminine. Every person has a feminine and a masculine side. Our spirit opens into the Infinite and receives its inspiration and direction from the Infinite.

Never think of a person's body when healing, because the body is an effect. Treat only the mind. There is no disease unless there is a thought image of that disease in the mind. When the thought image is removed, the disease cannot exist.

We are all surrounded by an aura—a mental atmosphere, or subjective mind. This aura may be easily seen by some people or by anyone if concentration is used. The aura of some people projects from the body about three inches while with others it fills the entire room. Two people come together and feel each other's aura, or subjective mind, and they instantly like or dislike the person whose aura they feel.

Thought is the substance of a thing. Thoughts are things. Every object in the universe is the result of a thought expressed. Subjective mind is divine principle, psychic power, subjective law, God, and surrounds us always. A practitioner's work begins and ends within him- or herself. Everything—ability, race experience, talent, et cetera—is potential in subjectivity. Treatment is clear seeing, clearing out, realizing the truth—knowing that all is all right and good. When the inner consciousness agrees with our outer world, sees it as the good that it is, we shall realize our desires. Subjective consciousness is largely made up of race suggestion and prenatal influence. Life had no beginning; it was with God, but form has a beginning. Form may have many changes. Through the proper use of the subjective law, if you do not neutralize it by mental suggestion, you can bring that to pass which you can think.

Unity

Life is all or nothing. There is no such thing as an absent treatment. No such thing as transmitted thought. It is in the last analysis a thought created in Universal Mind, in Mind which is everywhere present.

When giving a treatment, treat until all doubt is gone from your thought. Realize that the thing is done. Then rest absolutely satisfied and positive that that thing is done. Wisdom and understanding of the law places us in a position to heal and demonstrate, and become teachers.

Law is Mind in action. This comprehends all law; for what the physicist calls physical laws are all mental laws. A thought exists until it accomplishes its purpose since the subjective, the Infinite, can only deduce, cannot deny us anything. You can depend impersonally upon Unity.

Your objective draws its life, its attractiveness, its health, from the subjective. The objective is the expression of your thought. You can only know the truth in you. The possibility of demonstration does not depend upon conditions, time, opportunity, environment; it depends entirely on you. There is no waiting upon principle; all may happen instantly. All that happens to us, happens through us.

God is neither good nor bad, but just is. There is nothing but freedom in the Universe. If you are sick, that expresses your freedom. You are as free as your thought. You never deal with conditions; you deal with mind. Disease is a mental image, and nothing else, a state of consciousness.

Never treat people for disease, poverty, or unhappiness, but build up a consciousness that there is no loss, no want, no wrong, no disease. If you remove the thought of disease and want, no disease and want can exist, because there is no thought to give it life. The basis of all misery, want, lack, sorrow, poverty, and disease is a belief in duality. This belief in duality must be absolutely rejected and forgotten forever.

All life is a mental picture. Think of your life as a game. It is nothing but a game. Forget all your worries, your wants, disease. To do this, first cleanse the subjective mind; clear it out so that the Infinite or Spirit Life may flow through the medium, or in order that inspiration from the Infinite may flow through you.

The subconscious mind is conscious of itself and of what is within itself and of what you tell it; and it is always acting upon what you tell it. In our subjectivity we are one with All upon what you tell it. In our subjectivity we are one with all subjective thought. Ideas all represent identities. You cannot deal in generalities; therefore, you must be specific.

Question: How do I treat myself?

Ernest Holmes: If you are a beginner, treat aloud, in order to avoid intruding thoughts which you do not desire, and also to avoid falling asleep. Learn to concentrate not by effort, but easily by bringing back to the mind particular thought, on which you desire to concentrate. Repeatedly bring the attention to the desired thought, and you will have accomplished concentration before you know it. Lack of proper concentration is the cause of all the trouble in life.

There is no good and bad, no human and divine, no God and—something else—no sickness and health, no wealth and poverty.

The something which makes you sick also makes you well, and

the thing which makes you well also makes you sick. This teaches and proves that nothing opposes you. This thing heals you as quickly as it makes you sick and makes you sick as quickly as it heals you. Never have a sense that you are working against anything. There is and can be no opposition, except in your own thought. There is nothing in the universe but cause and effect. Nothing opposes you. God cannot deny us; nothing can deny us except ourselves. The Universe cannot deny you anything. All things in the Universe are subject to you. You are the *truth*, all of it, the total truth, not a part of it. There is no more truth and no other truth than *you*.

The Universe takes us at our own valuation and cannot take us any other way. We are the evolved personality of God—God personified.

Don't struggle after anything. Think of the great omniscient mind as knowing just the particular thing that you want to know and that you can know now, that thing which is in the Infinite or omniscient mind for you. There is no power in the flesh or out of it that can influence you except good. Thought knows itself to be the power that it is, and it knows itself to be the only power there is. The feminine principle, the subjective, receives all thoughts and starts to work on them just as the soil receives all seeds and starts them growing. The subjective state of mind is far the greater and more important because it is the creative power.

Healing

Question: Why don't people get better results in their healing work?

Ernest Holmes: The reason people do not get better results is that they do not understand that there is a principle which works independently of anybody, even of themselves. All of our treating and all of our mental work should be done from an impersonal standpoint. Truth demonstrates itself. We don't have to prove it to be true. A treatment takes place in yourself, in your own mind. A practitioner never has to think outside of himself. It is not necessary for us to entertain in our thought that we have to treat anything outside of ourselves.

Question: What is meant by Divine Principle?

Ernest Holmes: Divine Principle means that we are part of and surrounded by an Infinite Mind which is the only actor. Nothing moves but mind. It is as though every one of us were in one common mind and brought down to a point of personified consciousness.

There is one common mind at the root of everyone's personality. There is one common mind in the universe. We all have a separate objective intellectual faculty, but at the bottom of this, there is one subjectivity in the universe and we all use it. Even vegetables use it. For example, say we are a row of individual cabbages. We are rooted in one soil and air. What the cabbage is to be, is the power that comes through its use, just like a fish in water or like a sponge. You are in it and it is in you.

Every disease that appears in the body must come up through mind into that body. When that life principle which you are deserts your body and your body remains what you call a corpse, then your body no longer gets sick, so that while you let go of yourself, you see that the body gets sick. It could not get sick unless there is an intelligence to cognize the trouble.

Consider a contagious disease. It is physically contagious between living people, but it is not contagious between dead people. We must remember that there is just one subjective mind in the universe. This is a point people do not get. They cannot seem to see how it is that they can treat a person without touching. If there is but one subjective mind in the universe, it can be nothing but receptive, plastic, neutral, impersonal, creative; and as you impress upon it a certain thought, it is the actor.

Here lies the difference between mental suggestion and healing from principle. A person who is treating through mental suggestion is treating for the idea. That is hypnotic force and when you hypnotize, mind is withdrawn. This patient will return to his own condition. That which you call your subjectivity is the point of attraction in Universal Mind which brings it up. The only thing which binds us is the only thing that frees us. Bondage is freedom. Love and hate are one attitude. Fear and faith are the same attitude.

They are one mind, one mental attitude. There are only different ways of using it to cause it to be manifested.

One can think into mind-diseased thoughts. For example, what are the metaphysical reasons for the flu? They are fear, confusion, and suggestion. The fear of all people during the war and confusion are what brought it on. Fear is at the base of all fever. Disease is an impersonal thought force. Thought is the only activity of consciousness. It is the movement of mind upon itself. It is involution.

Thought Force is the result of the movement of this consciousness which sets forth a law. Thought is a definite, specific thing. We must get the wrong thought out of us. Disease is the image of thought held in the mind until it appears in the body. Train your thoughts in peace and harmony and you will not get sick. Think peace, health, and harmony and you are always well. First comes intelligence, then comes the movement or action displayed in the body or matter. First there is the subjective state of thought, and then it comes out in physical expression.

We did not at one time have an objective consciousness. We are born from subjectivity into objectivity. Consider the baby; when it comes into the world, it is purely subjective. It has no perception nor thought processes. It just lives instinctively. It came out of subjectivity into objectivity. As soon as it comes into objectivity, the brain develops. You know a child does not gain its objective faculties as soon as an animal. Human beings are slower than animals but gain deeper intelligence. From the beginning, the human body is forming an objective consciousness. Everything and everybody is born from a perfect condition and takes on objectivity. It brings along with it subjectivity, certain tendencies. It brings very few diseases. It inherits very little. It, however, inherits subjective receptivity toward a belief in such things as disease. As they objectify, they begin to imagine they see things. From the first they are happy, free, spontaneous, live instinctively, and are naturally correct. Children will instinctively give correct answers to questions asked them. It is natural to tell things just as they are. They do not know anything different. They are always correct. Then, as they get older, they contact life. They hear about struggle, death, divorce, marriage, and they begin to think. They shove back the subjectivity and accept emotions and observe the objective.

Question: What is law?

Ernest Holmes: Law is law; it is impersonal. When you understand that statement in its truest sense, you will see there is nothing to oppose you.

Question: What is race suggestion?

Ernest Holmes: It is a great deal more than people think it is. It means that in this great race consciousness of mind, this great psychic life in which we are immersed, there is thought form, and thought image and mental equivalents of everything that has happened since the race began, which has not been neutralized by a direct opposite force. Disease comes three-fourths from race suggestion. Positive-minded, sharply individualized people throw off diseases. It is those who are not afraid who are never sick.

Do not treat the patient as a sick body. If you do, you are treating the body. We don't treat the body because the body is effect and not cause. Bodies and conditions never move but are moved upon. There are degrees to which the mind can become adjusted to harmony in the universe. We live subject to the race laws of disease and poverty until we ourselves free ourselves from it. If you express any disease, you are expressing an affirmation of life along which you have allowed it to flow.

Question: What does the term *treatment* mean?
Ernest Holmes: There are three forms of treatment.

I. Christian Science teaches two methods. One is the process of affirmation and denials. The other is the argumentative method. Argument of itself is not the thing that does the work, but by arguing we build up within ourselves a realization of our thought sinking into subjectivity which neutralizes the thought about the person acted upon as being so and so.

2. Divine Science takes out all denials. It recognizes affirmations only. They say we are the substance of God. Their belief embodies all of denial because affirmation and denial are just the same.

3. Healing by meditation. The practitioner takes one thought and holds it until he or she gets a clear realization and vision of the truth is experienced. We meditate on the truth and think and think until we see the truth, there is nothing but the truth, nothing to deny or oppose it.

When you are treating a patient, you have no personal responsibility for the recovery of that patient. You are not healing the patient. You are setting out in an impersonal, receptive mind certain statements which this one mind is going to carry into effect through the patient.

The practitioner must have a clear vision in order to heal. The mind knows the person who is being treated. The subconscious, but not the unconscious, mind does the work. Subconsciousness does not mean unconscious. Never hold yourself as a conscious personality when treating. Believe that all the consciousness backs up what you say.

Disease will be healed, provided you get at the cause of it and remove it, and provided the individual for whom you are working is willing to surrender up the cause, and provided the disease has not reached such a stage that your perception of wholeness is not enough to neutralize all the wrong that is connected with it. Never look at disease. Unearth the mental cause. Don't see them physically as a sick person. See them as a student, as a perfect being, a perfect God, a perfect person and they are healed.

In treating someone in your own home, there is a tendency to let sympathy enter in personal thought concerning the patient. Deal with principle only, barring everything else. Give your treatment, forget it. Don't think of the patient again until the next time you treat. Come to a realization of an impersonal force when treating. Have no personal sense of responsibility. Subjective thoughts are stronger during sleep than when one is awake, because the physical and objective faculties are at repose.

Question: How do we treat to remove fear?
Ernest Holmes: Sin is the root of all fear and trouble. I realize myself to be the perfect manifestation of truth; I am one in the Infinite Mind by reason of the fact that there is but one Mind and in order to be all, there must be nothing between this Infinite Mind and myself. I recognize myself as being complete, total, and perfect. In spite of any fear, in spite of any foolishness, I am yet absolutely perfect. That thing which calls itself fear has no ground for the opinion. The one perfect mind is my Mind now. In this one Mind I am healed and known as a perfect, complete, limitless, intelligent, radiant, strong, vital, and divine being. There is that in

me which recognizes this thing. There is that in me which is open and receptive to this great perfect life.

Question: How is absent treatment possible?

Ernest Holmes: We recognize that everything is Universal Mind and that nothing moves but Mind. Intelligence is back of everything acting through force which is concrete, definite, and real. The reason why people do not more plainly discern that mental healing is possible is because people do not understand the meaning of causation. If it were not true that we all have one common Mind, mental or metaphysical healing would be absolutely impossible except through hypnotic suggestion—which is not the way in which it is done at all. If everybody had a separate mind, this thing that we are talking about would be impossible. There is but one fundamental Intelligence in the universe which has given rise to every controversy in the world. We recognize unity and not duality. There is but one common Mind and one mind common to everybody. This Mind manifests itself through us. Mind is an individualized center of God consciousness. All law is Mind in action. Every disease that you have must come to your mind. Psychologists simply recognize that everything that they have ever learned about this subjective thought is simply a statement about the way subjective mind works through them. Is it perfectly clear to you that there is but one subjective mind in the universe and that it is the base of health and disease, even though the disease may be personified through you? It is upon this understanding alone that absent treatment is possible. Healing takes place entirely on a subjective plane.

Question: Is it the subjective or creative mind, or is it the consciousness of God?

Ernest Holmes: No, of course not. It is the spirit and the soul of the universe, a dual nature of that which is one. It is the Intelligence within us which teaches us how to deal with it which is God. That thing is subject to that Intelligence. Those who intend to heal as a profession will have to take up further study along these lines. They should study psychology and subjective consciousness.

Mind is in us and we are in Mind. Out of this Mind through us comes everything that is. Every disease then is an image of thought held in Mind until it appears in the body. We must first have a suggestive picture in Mind. It is not always a direct image. For instance, while every disease is an effect and must have a suggestive cause, the suggestive cause nine times out of ten is the consciousness in the thought of the person who has it. It is true that every disease has a direct prototype in the subjective mind. It is also true that the individual who suffers the disease nine times out of ten never thought that he or she would have that disease. Healing is accomplished when somebody realizes the law and speaks a word to set in motion a law to neutralize the image of the disease held in Mind which ails the individual who is suffering from it.

For example, John Smith has a cancer of the stomach. That is a most common ailment which many people seem to have. He does not know what made him sick. Of course there is no physical basis for disease. He has confidence enough to come to the practitioner and ask for healing. He does not know a thing about his own nature. Probably he would become antagonistic over any suggestion about the truth of his own nature. He would say: "I have no faith in your method of treatment, but I am willing to be helped." That attitude of mind is perfectly fair. I would be more willing to deal with a person of that kind than one who is unwilling and also has no faith. Never argue with anybody. Always accept the truth as you know it. This practitioner knows this thing is mental. He knows that not only is that disease mental but it is held in this one universal subjectivity. He knows that disease is simply an impersonal thought force operating through whatever channel it may find a place to operate in. He knows that since there is nothing but Mind in the universe, he is not dealing with the physical body nor trying to heal a physical condition. He does not attempt to manifest or do anything to his individual body.

Some people think they have to put their hand on the individual to get results. Forget it. Magnetism is the transmission of vital energy from one body to another. A magnetic healer may help individuals until worn out and then the patients go away and for a time seem healed but get sick again. We don't deal with magnetic healing. We treat that person not as a patient, not as a diseased body, nor as a physical body. We must not think of disease as connected or a part of the person at all. A practitioner is simply stating right out in Mind what is wanted for that person definitely, and the one who is the most definite, the most positive will be the best healer.

A practitioner knows that he is putting in the mind of John Smith a perfect idea of a perfect spirit or God. We get that impression of Smith as being absolutely perfect. But that is not enough. There is a definite something which heals Smith. If it is held in subjective mind that he has a cancer, this practitioner has got to clean out of his own thought any belief that Smith has a cancer. If the practitioner is successful in healing his own thought, which is absolutely necessary, there will be no doubt but that there will be a healing in John Smith. It goes into Mind and comes up at the level of recognition.

A practitioner who succeeds in inducing within his own subjective state of thought a recognition of the perfect will always find it externalized in the body of the patient, provided that patient is receptive to truth. The practitioner keeps in mind that this thing is infinite, universal, omnipresent, creative, plastic, and deductive only.

Back of this thought of disease there is a great deal more than there seems to be. There is race suggestion and race thought. In this treatment, in as far as you know how, you take up every broken law. In as far as you see clearly, you examine every line. There is a belief that we are born in sin and conceived in iniquity.

If you can succeed in removing all of these obstructions, you will be sure to heal your patient. This thing is an absolute and exact science and cannot help but work. There are not very many good healers. It is because they do not do their work properly. Principle has to work through us. There is no way to wholesale a treatment. Every case is a special, individualized, personified thing in Mind. Everyone has at the base of their life one common Mind. Talk to the patient if possible. Explain the law and ascertain from him the things that ail him; and you will find nine times out of ten that the ailments will be in some way related to the emotions.

A practitioner is one who recognizes the fact that there is nothing but one Universal Mind in motion. That all disease is an image of thought held in Mind until it appears in the body. They are successful who consciously speak from their objective mind into subjectivity and know directly the thing that they want done.

If you find that John Smith has a cancer, that the cause of it is long grief, then you have to go remove that sense of grief. Just saying "John Smith has no cancer" will not do it. Mental work has to be done if you want to accomplish results. I don't mean work hard.

I don't mean compel something to happen. Practitioners must always have peace of mind. There must always be an inner sense of calm which comes from the recognition that they are dealing with Omniscience, Omnipotence, that which is perfect and complete. Now be conscious when you speak a word to the Mind. Don't argue with anybody but get to work and think. Be conscious. Say that Smith recognizes his perfection. You begin to give your treatment. Of course you realize that he is born of Spirit and not of matter. There must be the recognition that he is born of Spirit and now is Spirit. With that recognition comes the pure, holy, undefiled, uncontaminated consciousness. The idea of sin will be removed from Mind. This word which you speak frees him from every suggestion and he is healed.

Impersonal force is going around seeking whom it may devour. Suppose you sat down and treated a person. About the first thing that will come to you will be a hypnotic thought which will say to you: You can't do it. That thing is not you. It is this impersonal thought trying to operate through you and tell you that you cannot do it. You must at once declare you are freed from hypnotic suggestion and illusion. In order that you may know that you are concrete and definite, get the feeling of the truth of what you say. If it is done in mind, it will get results. Know that you are doing things as definitely as a gardener knows that he is making a garden, and knows that vegetables or flowers will come up when he plants a seed. Know the things that you say are true. Be definite.

Next comes the doubt in your mind as to whether or not you understand. This is the same imperfect thing which comes fundamentally, perhaps, from a belief that you have to do the healing yourself. You will not say "I am not good enough to heal" or "I don't know enough to heal," when you know that the thing you are talking about is God. Mind is the only actor that there is. There is not law but Mind. Nothing moves but Mind. Back of everything is Infinite Intelligence. So then, all this argument is a lie, pure and simple. A lie is that which is not the truth, and that which is not the truth you are not afraid of because it is not. Therefore, it is a false claim. You will not entertain false claims. Know that you are dealing with the truth. Know that you know. If everyone in the world says you can't, nevertheless, it is true that you can. Nothing can deny the truth. Just think of it as a joke when such a statement is made. It is the truth that wins out.

Know how to heal. If a patient comes to you and says "I don't know what ails me. I don't feel good. Do you think you can help me any?" just say, "Yes, I can heal you." Study your patient. Don't make a physical diagnosis of your patient. Study in order to get correspondence and comparison. Suppose a person who has heart trouble comes to you for healing. You know that the heart of itself cannot get sick, any more than the heart of itself can love. It is simply a physical organ through which Mind works. You are simply sizing up the situation in order to get at the thought force behind the person. Then, and not until then, do you come to the treatment. You forget the body entirely and are absent from the body and present in Mind. You will discover that back of this is a sense of fear. You should begin definitely to remove fear. There is a true saying that perfect love casts out all fear. The consciousness of the patient, which is the subjective state of thought in Mind, must come to see that everything is love, harmony, and perfect peace. You must come to see it for the patient first. If you can cover the patient with more love than he has fear, there will be a healing every time.

Every disease can be traced to a definite cause. All disease is mental. Heal through the Mind. Very few people, when asking for a treatment, will come right out and tell the exact truth about themselves. Psychoanalysis is the process which makes them tell the whole truth. If the analysis is successful, the healing is bound to follow.

When you are giving a treatment, you are thinking. You are definitely thinking, and you know that you will meet opposition, obstruction, suppression, fear, doubt, failure, everything morbid, and emotion. Every time your thought hits one, it no longer exists; it is obliterated and it is no more. The person who is clever enough to make the patient come through, can always heal without a question of a doubt.

Question: Why doesn't God heal?

Ernest Holmes: Because God has made us and let us alone. We are independent. We will be sick until we get tired of being sick. That's all.

If your thought looks big, it is big. Everything looks just as you see it. Pictures are taken of thought forms. Thoughts are things and practitioners must recognize that their thoughts hit the nail on the head. Suppose a person is in severe pain. The thing that will heal is the realization of peace which will give relief immediately. With a patient who has fever, the first thing you must absolutely do is to remove from the atmosphere all fear. The fever will disappear from the body of the patient as soon as confidence and peace and love are established to eliminate fear. Then sit there until the fever is gone. The patient is suffering when the practitioner sits down and neutralizes and destroys it all. Then the patient is surprised.

Question: How do we begin in this practice of healing of a patient?

Ernest Holmes: Clean out the atmosphere of the patient's room. If there is a family who fears for him, you have got to surround him with the protection against the fear thoughts of the family. The family must be cleared from the patient's thoughts first and then work on the patient.

Disease has no government. It is a coward that will flee before the truth. There is nothing but the truth. There is nothing else. There is no limitation imposed upon us. Your mind must always be peaceful. You must know the thing you are doing is definite, dynamic, complete, and it will work. Don't let fear come into thought. Treat yourself first before going to the patient. Talk to yourself. Adopt a general method of treatment. The best method for a beginner is to go through a system of affirmations and denials at first. It is simple, and you can see it plainly. Then later, when you are sure you see the truth as it is, and you know that you know, the affirmations and denials will merge in one.

Everything is mental and is transferred to a certain plane. We know that nothing can come up through our consciousness into objectivity but such thoughts as we claim. Mrs. Eddy, founder of Christian Science, first taught these things with a certain degree of clearness. She said: "If to argue in mind in such a manner as to heal a person will heal, then it must follow that arguing in the opposite way will make a person sick and such practice is known as malpractice."

General Form of a Treatment

1. Recognize your own perfection.
2. Then build up the recognition of perfection in your patient.

3. Then directly attack the thought form of the thing
   that ails the patient, recognizing that this word oblit-
   erates and completely destroys that thing.
4. Then finish our treatment with the great realization
   of peace and feel it is done. Recognize that it is done.
   When you know your treatment is done, or when you
   feel the truth, you yourself will gradually find that
   you feel a sense of great peace.

Question: What do we do when someone comes to us and says:
"I have had a terrible misunderstanding with a great friend of
mine. We don't speak to each other."

Ernest Holmes: This is not a normal state of being. It is not
right. Now don't think you have to hypnotize your friend. What is
that misunderstanding? What is the fundamental basic error which
has produced this misunderstanding? It is the lack of the realization of unity. It is a belief in duality. A thought is true to you
when based upon this one principle which you know is true. There
is nothing but Intelligence. There is a process of reasoning and
elimination which approaches truth so that you will be able to dis-
criminate between truth and false teaching.

What is it that separated these people? They are not separate
in consciousness. There has come up an impersonal belief in separation which is founded on a belief in duality. We all exist in each
other.

Be controlled by God. Free yourself from all illusions. We are
not a part of the truth; we are all the truth there is.

Question: What would you do if you had broken bones in your
body?

Ernest Holmes: I would just have them set. Our understanding is not sufficient to set bones. There is no limitation which principle imposes upon us. We can only go as far as we know. Principle is Infinite, but until we can demonstrate, we use any method.

Question: How did you rid yourself of glasses?†

Ernest Holmes: I got a mental equivalent of the great vision. I said: "There is one vision and it is looking through me. There is just one vision and it is working through me and it is working with absolute perfection." When my concept conceived of that vision as looking clearly and perfectly through me, the specific cause was removed.

Question: How would you treat for self-confidence in anything we might undertake?

Ernest Holmes: Get away from the objective sense of things and realize the great subjective consciousness of life from which everything comes; herein dwells God alone, peace. This treatment is to free every one of us from the belief in bondage, no matter what that bondage may be. This treatment recognizes in every one of us that we are a pure and perfect idea, a perfect and total and complete expression of almightiness and of Infinite Life. We know that this word which knows itself to be the presence and the power and the activity of omniscience, irresistibly, completely and absolutely destroys every thought unlike itself and every thought of fear and bondage is swept away; and every sense of limitation and every idea of it, whether we be conscious that it is there or not, is now rendered null and forever void of expres-

---

† Mr. Holmes wore glasses for years and could not see without them.

sion as this word reaches out and destroys it. Truth is back of truth which knows itself to be and it is radiant; and we know that we know; and the one eternal mind in us knows that it is; and we know that we are it. It perceives that every fear is removed and faith and confidence and peace we are conscious of alone.

Dealing with
Conditions in Life

Out of all the people who seek to demonstrate prosperity, very few people do it. We are surrounded by a psychic life, a subjective, creative, conscious, receptive, neutral, and plastic force which receives the impress of our thought always and has no alternative. You will find that whether you are conscious of it or not, every one of us is right where we are because of what we are, because of what we now are and of what the world believes about us. Recognition of this is necessary. Don't deny it. Everyone is right where they are because of what they are.

Recognizing that we are what we are because of that which we are gives us a basis upon which to work in order that we may become something of which we do not now appear to be. We have to self-analyze ourselves. The principle of this is universal subjectivity, or universal receptivity, and is the stuff out of which everything is made. This is law. It is an immutable law. It has to be exact. Feel that your mind at once takes up this concept and works upon it. When you treat, feel that something is actually happening, no matter how great a responsibility lies in the thing that is to be done. Every demonstration must be made in peace and confidence and in the realization of the divine love and perfection as permeating everything. It is the law of correspondence, cause and effect.

People say: "I can't demonstrate prosperity." You must know that you are dealing with a substance that made everything. People, animals, donkeys, grass, and everything that is. Nothing moves but mind. You are dealing with a mind that is. In your concept you are not dealing with a business or environment, but you are creating firsthand the thing that you want done. Visualize it.

The most important thing that we want to recognize is that God is our supply. It is hard to get that recognition. We believe in faith, but we cannot realize that our supply is in God. The trouble is not that we are not doing enough, but that we don't know enough. Understand the law through which it works. Truly and consciously speak the thing that you want and then see it. It is at once taken up by Mind.

The Law of Mental Equivalents

You realize a man who has never had a dollar in his life cannot demonstrate a million dollars. A person who never had anything like that cannot comprehend it. If a million dollars came to him it wouldn't be recognized because he does not know the value, or that there is any value. It would not be recognized after it was received. If a man couldn't think a million dollars, he would never get it. I don't mean see it, but think it.

It is impossible to demonstrate a million dollars. You cannot sit down and think that you have a million dollars. It is not through this process that you get it. We must clear out of our consciousness every thought of lack and limitation. Clear out all the race suggestion of limitation, and the belief in poverty and lack, and that belief that "I have to work for a living." These things hypnotize people and bind them. The whole thing is impersonal. We don't work to earn a living. You must de-hypnotize yourself. Don't acknowledge bondage. We don't have to work. It is asked: "If everyone would do that, who would do the work?" There will be such an evolution and such proof that there would be very little work to be done. An active thought will always be active in body, but you can free your consciousness from the bondage of having to work for a living. This thought is absolutely desirable and commendable. Specifically, every day take the time to declare that that Spirit which is you, lives in you, and your consciousness recognizes itself to be without limitation; it is perfect, complete, free, unbound.

We induce a mental state and after we have induced a mental state in the subjective, it is clear what will happen; for the subjective cannot induce but can only deduce. We induce, Mind produces. A person involves consciousness intelligence. Mind evolves. The trouble with most of us is that while we are speaking an objective word, we have to free our inner consciousness of that thing which holds us. When you treat, you realize all that. Then you realize that here you are in Mind and you are speaking right out into Mind. Mind is the actor. Your demonstration will depend on you. You have got to have a mental equivalent of everything you are going to get. The thing which is induced, involved, can only evolve at the level of its concept. So each of us has to start right where we are.

Suppose a man is working for fifty dollars a week. He knows what fifty dollars a week is. He already has a mental equivalent of fifty dollars a week. Mental equivalent means that there is something in him which knows that fifty dollars a week is all that he needs to clothe him and his family and supply his needs. He has not got the mental equivalent that he could spend three times as much. He set a price on himself. This man cannot conceive of one hundred dollars a week, and it is absolutely useless for him to sit down and try to demonstrate it. He has got to grow in his own consciousness. He must realize plenty and free his consciousness of limitation. Gradually he conceives of earning more; and as he grows, he can easily conceive of one thousand dollars a week. He could speak an audible word which would be substantiated by a just realization. When he gets accustomed to one thousand dollars a week, then automatically the thing grows. He comprehends more. He can think bigger things. There must always be peace of mind, a contentment, a harmonious consciousness. The activity of mind is the eternal expression of itself.

It is possible for each one of us to financially free ourselves. Start right where you are. Suppose you are in business. Just a little business. You have from ten to twenty customers a day and you sell about fifty dollars' worth of goods, getting about thirty dollars' gross profit. You can live on this, you say. You are satisfied. You who are in such a condition are not going to demonstrate that you run a department store. You must first realize that there is no limitation. Realize that you have and are getting more and more trade. Always demonstrate ahead and not behind. If you plant a seed in the ground, there is something that will make the seed grow. We call it Mind.

Here is a man, and he desires a certain thing; we call this a habit. He hates someone and wants to kill him. He thinks and thinks, and an irresistible power obsesses him and he goes and does it. That is the way habits are formed. If a man wants prosperity and provides a mental equivalent, sooner or later an impersonal force will irresistibly bring about his desires, and he will realize prosperity. That is what we call demonstration. It does not depend on any environment, location, people, or anything of that kind. It depends on you.

Going back to the man who has the little business, let us say that he begins to conceive of more activity. He has understood the law. He treats himself. He declares that right here there radiates activity, an atmosphere of positive attraction, and surely he has customers. It is the atmosphere of attraction that makes you want to buy something in a store although you had no idea of purchasing when you entered the store.

Sit down each day and mentally see people coming in your store and purchasing, just like the man with the little store. When you get a clear picture of that thing, visualize the thing. Turn it right over to universal subjectivity and it is done. It always says: "I will."

Question: How would you demonstrate prosperity by absent treatment?

Ernest Holmes: Suppose someone said: "I want a position." You sit down in Mind and realize that this word which is being spoken is being spoken for that person. Realize and see the specific definite law. You have got to operate that law. You realize that this person has this position. Declare right in mind what you want mind to do for this person. How would you do it? You would do it just exactly the way you want it done. Don't do it the way you don't want it done, because you will get what you don't want. The one thing that people have got to learn is that they are dealing with Intelligence. There is nothing but principle and our use of the word for that person just when you want it to happen. You are really inducing within your own consciousness a concept which deduces that which is true about the person whom you are treating, and evolves it or externalizes it. The person is thus and so. Mind takes it up and agrees with that and does it.

Question: How would you treat five people who came to you and they all wanted prosperity?

Ernest Holmes: They all want one definite thing, prosperity. If you declare this word and they all get into one unified consciousness, it is true that they will receive just such prosperity to the degree that they accept it. You will find in healing people of poverty that they need to be analyzed.

Question: How would you sell a piece of property?

Ernest Holmes: That is a concrete manifestation of subjective consciousness. Speak right into Mind and you know that this divine intelligence surrounds you. It knows of the person who wants that property. You speak that in Mind. Mind is a unit and one. Somewhere there is someone who wants it. Through Mind at once, you are connected with that person and your physical correspondent is brought about. Intelligence will bring it to you. Know that intelligence has brought this person to you. Always affirm that it is so. Just know that the person who wants it is connected with you. The thing that you are dealing with, the thing that made the Universe, is this thing you are dealing with. There is nothing but it. If you can induce within yourself a mental equivalent upon consciousness, you are bound to get a complete demonstration. What is it that says "It can't be done"? It is an imperfect thought force, race suggestion, belief in limitation; these cause it.

If you meet a successful man, you will find that this man has a consciousness of success. He never talks about poverty and limitation. If you meet a man who is not a success, He is always talking about failure. Don't let people talk to you about failure. If a man wants to be sick and poverty stricken, that is his own business.

Question: How often should you treat? What is a treatment?

Ernest Holmes: A treatment is inducing upon your subjective a state of thought. A treatment is complete when the induction is complete. Do it until you know it is done. Do it until the answer is yes. I would treat, not with a lack of confidence, but with a sense of treating until it is done and you know it is done. Principle never fails. We often fail to live up to it.

Every movement we make in Mind is immutable. Every day my concept becomes clearer and clearer until at last all these things that hinder it are neutralized and the one thing in Mind comes out; that is why we repeat. We state every day that we know thus and thus is so, and it gradually comes out. All negatives must be neutralized. By repeating this thing, we are always treating ourselves. Just as rapidly as we think, there is a certain something that happens. We have to think until we see clearly.

Silence Demonstration

Now we realize that we are dealing with the one perfect principle. God is all that there is and there is none else, only one, nothing else but God. God is life and God is our life now. Now we know that we dwell within this perfect state of being which is conscious only of perfection and we know that the law of our life is conscious only of that which is perfect and the law of life is the law of our thought, of our mind, which is the law of God in us. We know that every thought or belief in limitation is by this word removed from us and from around us. We know that that thing which calls itself poverty and limitation and sickness and lack is simply a false belief, and we know we no longer believe it; and we know that it is not, cannot operate through us or in us, cannot find any corresponding thought within us. We know only freedom and we know that this word which we speak now wipes out every false sense of limitation and erases it from our consciousness. We know we are dealing with the one perfect thing which speaks to our thought, gives of itself freely, and is without limitation and so we perceive that there is no law of false belief, nothing in us or around us that can hinder truth from entering our consciousness. Now we realize that all is perfect; and we see and know and Mind in us knows and realizes that all that there is is flowing through us. We conceive of our selves as embodying all activity and all power and all life and all supply. There is nothing that conceives of limitation. This is a perfect and complete word, and it knows itself to be the power of that Infinite Law. It is itself that thing which it claims to be. Conceive of yourself as now having embodied that thing which you desire. Every living one of us knows itself to be a divine, positive, strong, radiant, complete, individualized manifestation of God. We declare that every physical instrument is adequate and perfect through which Mind works and that our word wipes out every false cause of limitation and recognizes only freedom and it is so.

Question: How would you treat to increase a class in music?

Ernest Holmes: You want to get more students. It is definite in your mind. First of all you recognize that there is limitless power. You are making yourself say that. There is nothing but activity. You have induced within yourself that there is nothing but activity. Intelligence has brought to you everybody who desires this thing which you have. Your consciousness flows out in everybody and everywhere. You know that there are people somewhere who are looking for that thing which you have, and that unity which you have established draws them in. You do not have to make things happen. Neither do you have to work out the details. Intelligence gives you details. Depend upon principle alone, and principle produces to you the thing you want.

A teacher came to me about three years ago and said: "No one comes to my studio. I have nothing, I have no money and I have a piano that is not paid for." She went through the treatment as above. Things began to happen. She said she had many students and couldn't go in a cafe but what if somebody was there who wanted to take lessons.

Question: Can you tell always when you have the right "hunch"?

Ernest Holmes: No you cannot always tell. Our life is not clear mentally to know when we are right. We are generally apt to get the right hunch. If I go into a business proposition, I go very imperfectly about it. Divine Intelligence directs me just what to do about this proposition.

The one underlying subjective principle of deduction and creative consciousness which is substance, which is the stuff that everything comes out of, that will show your consciousness the method of procedure. In any case, the only thing that there is, is Intelligence, substance, and form. Here is a limitless intelligence, self-consciousness, and within this limitless intelligence is a limitless substance which is the form of everything and appears in space. In this limitless intelligence and substance and form, the form is dissolvable back into substance as intelligence acts and reacts through it to produce it. That is the spirit and soul and body of the universe, the unity of everything. All substance is unified. When it is dissolved, it is one primal substance. We are one. We are made in the image and likeness of God and the matter is made out of dirt. One is involution and the other is evolution. One is cause and other effect. You can't have a consciousness without a creativeness.

If you want to demonstrate prosperity, you must have a consciousness of prosperity. If you want to demonstrate activity, you must have a consciousness of activity. No matter what we are or what we want to demonstrate, we must have a consciousness of that thing. Certain thoughts produce certain things, and an opposite thought neutralizes it and like thought adds to it.

Question: Are we one with Infinite Mind?

Ernest Holmes: We are not one with Infinite Mind, but one *in it.* Do you see the difference? We are in it; we are not with it. If you say "I am one with the Infinite Mind," there is a subtle sense of God and you. There is no separation if you say "I am in God." Whether you think it objectively or whether you think it subjectively, you are thinking in God. The objective thought leaves the brain and goes into expression. There is no avoiding the thought that you are in God. There is nothing but immutability in the universe. We are Infinite in all capacity to think, to will, to wish.

Question: How would you treat a cigarette fiend?

Ernest Holmes: Now there is something about this habit that this man can't resist. He has used his willpower. The human willpower is not a creative thing. It is simply the mental ability to hold our thought in place. If a person has a habit, it is not best to tell them to resist and fight it. If they begin to fight it, they begin to affirm that it is, and they are doing largely the very thing they ought not to do. They are creating a condition until it becomes intensified. When they stop resisting it, it loosens up. If a person has a certain habit and it produces a definite disease, it is useless to treat for that disease unless the habit is removed. The world is not resisting you. You are resisting the world. If you want to heal yourself of the world's resistance to you, you have got to heal yourself of your resistance to it. It is clear from principle.

Question: Suppose a misunderstanding arises between two people. They have been friends for years. What can be done?

Ernest Holmes: Here is A and here is B. There comes in a misunderstanding, and B turns entirely away from A. Here is the question which everybody must decide for themselves: Have they a right to dissolve this thing? From my viewpoint, I say, "Yes." I believe absolutely that there should be perfect unity everywhere. B has turned completely away from A until there is a complete misunderstanding and separation. What are they going to do about it? In the first place, you and I know that their bodies did not turn away from each other. It is the permeating intelligence always which operates through the body. The separation is in mind and not in matter. If it is in mind, it is the only place to go to heal it. The separation is not in matter. No condition has arisen which could separate anything. Suppose two individuals say: "A condition arose which separates us." That is impossible. There may have arisen a condition which these individuals cognized and thought separated them, but that was not thought. What are you going to do to change that thing? You have got to erase in your mind, but what is this mind? You have got to erase in mind a concept that these two individuals are not one and if you succeed in erasing that concept, you will see from all objective observation that they are one. What you have got to do is to work yourself until you have mentally dissolved every idea of separation. This sense of separation is an illusion. It is a mistaken concept. As such it has no real

grounds of law governing it at all. So then declare that this word
which I speak dissolves any sense of separation which may be held
in Mind relative to these two individuals and establishes the recognition that there is but one Mind in which they are immersed until
in Mind or consciousness there is no longer any error and when
they have done that, nothing fails.

Question: May I always be absolutely sure that I can demonstrate?

Ernest Holmes: If you think you can't, I'll tell you why. It is because you think that you have to do it. When you realize there is
but one Mind in which you think or one Divine Principle, it is the
actor, and just as soon as you use the law, the law will operate for
you. You are learning to use a perfect, creative, deductive, neutral
force which will always respond because it is only deductive.

Question: How do you treat a boy who lies just as naturally and
easily as he tells the truth?

Ernest Holmes: I would treat him from the standpoint that nothing but the truth could operate through him. His consciousness
understands the truth. You will have not the least bit of difficulty
in bringing this out in the boy. I would not mistrust him. I would
have all the confidence in the world in him.

Question: Why do animals get sick?

Ernest Holmes: Animals do not preconceive diseases in Mind,
and yet they suffer from them. Do you deny the existence of bac-
teria? I affirm the existence of everything that seems to exist.
Animals are purely subjective, or almost entirely so. They have very
little objectivity or choice. Some animals have more than others.

Animals, generally speaking, very seldom get sick. Nature instinctively provides them with protection.

Question: Why did Jesus say "Go and tell no man"?

Ernest Holmes: Jesus recognized the law of psychology. A man was sick. He was healed. The sickness was a thought form, a belief. Jesus recognized that this man's consciousness was not equipped with the truth. If you are making demonstrations, keep it all to yourself unless you are working with someone who really understands it. That is why Jesus did it. Again Jesus said: "Go and sin no more lest a worse thing come upon you."

Question: Will this work have the same effect done verbally as if audibly?

Ernest Holmes: If we think or whisper or speak it, it doesn't matter. For the sake of clearness I believe that the ordinary beginner should at least say it to himself clearly because thought is form and word gives form to thought and Mind produces thought in things. So I would be very definite.

Question: Do you see any objection to cremation of the body?

Ernest Holmes: Not the slightest. There is a certain teaching that it takes just so long for the soul to spiral out of the body and the body should not be cremated for a certain length of time.

Success in Our
Environment and Personal
Relationships

Demonstration is not making something out of nothing. It is simply causing to appear in Mind a certain form, or manifestation of a concept. We will say that A, B, C, and D come to you as a practitioner. Now A is making fifteen dollars a week; B makes twenty-five dollars, C makes fifty dollars, and D makes two hundred dollars a week. The practitioner sees no difference between A, B, C, and D, only as four personalities in one Mind. The practitioner would speak the same word for all of them. The practitioner would say in Mind that they all want water and carries water to these people and fills their buckets. That is all a practitioner can do. They may direct this causation. Consciousness is Infinite and carries a totality of itself always with it. The practitioner then states in Mind that A, B, C, and D make a statement of their abundance. A practitioner gives exactly the same treatment to all of them. They are each provided with a consciousness through which the Infinite Mind flows. They have agreed that it is there and have accepted it. After it has gone out into manifestation, we see that A is getting fifteen dollars, B twenty-five dollars, C getting fifty dollars, and D is getting two hundred dollars a week. Why after the same power was set in motion did not A get two hundred dollars as well as D? A was not equipped to receive it. A had no mental equivalent for it. A's bucket was filled. That is where we often fall down. You can't transcend law. We have got to mentally equip ourselves to receive it. We have got to be in unity. You have to watch your thought force as carefully as you would watch the most valuable possession you have. It is all you have got. People's enemies are those of their own household [i.e., mind].

Suppose you go into a store. Nobody wants to wait on you. You get the right consciousness and you know it flows right through that place there. Remove every sense of antagonism and be at one with the universe; be dynamically one with the universe. Affirmatively, not negatively, actively go in your own consciousness and refuse to ever recognize any discouragement or any sense of lack. Refuse to recognize anything you don't want, no matter how arbitrary you may seem in doing it. You don't have to build up a lot of unnecessary antagonisms. In your own consciousness, in your own thought, recognize only that which you want to happen.

Suppose you are working on a problem and you don't know how to proceed. For instance, a man is in business. He doesn't know just how to go ahead. He wants information. He must first know definitely the thing he wants. Suppose he wants to know just how to do a certain thing. He must say that Divine Intelligence now informs him as to the method of procedure. There often comes a place when one doesn't know just which way to go. There are two or three things you might do, two or three positions you might accept, two or three businesses you might enter. You must recognize that divine intelligence decides just what course to take.

Subjectivity means beneath the threshold of objective consciousness. Subjectivity is not limited to anything. It is possible of everything. It can create anything. It inspires a writer, gives inspira-

tion to an inventor, helps a person and shows him how to advertise, or which business to go into. Always be definite. Suppose you
were in business and there were two papers in the town and you
wanted to advertise in one only. That is definite. I would definitely
state that Divine Intelligence knows in me which one of these papers is the one to use. Always be definite. The people who make
the best demonstrations are the ones who are the most definite.

Suppose an inventor came to you and said: "I am working on
a certain pattern to perfect a certain piece of machinery, and in
working it out, I can't seem to get one thing." You sit down with
him for a treatment. That is, you are going to concentrate your
thoughts on the one idea of wanting to produce this idea for him.
Every idea came out of every mind. Infinite consciousness directs
the way in which activity shall come out through us; therefore, it is
not a true statement to say anything "just happens."

If a person wants to draw a picture, or wants to build something, or wants to conceive of a new idea, there is that one thing
crowding out in expression; and it is so dynamic that it could open
up a brick walk just as a seed would break through in order for it to
grow. Mrs. Eddy, founder of Christian Science, said that Mind says
what it believes as truly as it believes what it says. If we want to get
an idea and go to a practitioner for help, the practitioner sits down
and delivers an idea from the Infinite. The thing that obstructs is
thought, not matter. There must be no obstruction. If a person
comes to you and says, "I am working on an invention. I can't seem
to get it," you sit down and go into the quiet and treat like this: Now
Smith is an inventor. Here is a certain idea trying to come through
him. Now there is nothing in him that can obstruct that idea. This
thing which is called lack of perception, this belief, that knowledge
is finite and human and limited, that whole thing is an illusion. In
your own consciousness you think and speak until the whole thing is

clear, and you conceive that limitless intelligence is occupying him. You state that this perfect idea is now in him; then he has it. In writing or inventing, or in business, or anything, it is the same way. It all works the same. Everything must be done from the spiritual basis.

Suppose a person came to you and said, "You know I have no friends, nothing comes my way. Everything I touch goes wrong. Everybody misunderstands me. I am very unhappy. I am alone in the world, et cetera, et cetera." You sit down to treat. This seems like a terrible thing that ails the patient but, as a matter of fact, it is nothing but an idea. You have to radiate in Mind about the patient and realize that all these ideas are not truth. You must be definite. Distinguish the patient from all others. If in absent treatment, never wonder as to the patient getting the treatment. You begin to radiate about this person. We are the center of Spirit, which recognizes itself as being all perfection. It recognizes itself as being the life of every living soul. Every living soul is one with John Smith; since Mind knows it and there is only one Mind, everybody's mind knows it. His mental attitude has succeeded at last in compelling everyone to know him. You can erase those thoughts which existed in him and cause to grow the thought that he is one with humanity. He will cause these things to enter his mind to the degree that he is mentally equipped. Entertain it and you are mentally equipped to give it. As you make your statements, you recognize that you are making them in Universal Mind, or Divine Principle, which is always the actor. You know that there is nothing that can hinder these things from working. You know that the thing you are dealing with is Principle, not personality, but that Principle will externalize through personality. If you can give a treatment knowing that Mind is the only actor, the only substance and intelligence and power that there is, and you know that Mind executes through you, you have no responsibility whatever except to do it.

It is just like a river flowing along. You stand on the bank. You put a boat in the water and the river carries the boat down. You don't have to carry the boat. There is not a person who has any duty to perform, or any God to please, or any obligation to meet. There is no obligation placed upon us by Divinity. The only reason that we are limited is because we have not allowed instinctive life to flow through us and because we said there is duality. If you are treating a person, have no sense of personal responsibility for making it happen. Through your word speak into Mind and know that Mind receives it. Mind believes, Mind accepts, Mind acts upon it, and Mind produces it.

Don't read about and don't talk to anybody about limitation. Don't read about divorce, murders, robberies, and accidents. As far as you are concerned, there are no such things. The newspapers are not fit to read. Read the *Literary Digest*; it gives you the best there is. Don't let horrid stories enter your consciousness. Go through a process of self-analysis. We are here, we are because of what we have done, because of the subjective that we allow to flow through us. Everything is impersonal. Size up the situation. If you lack, if you are poor, if you are without money, without the right position, if you are without all these things, don't fight anything. Just erase from your own consciousness anything that approaches a sense of lack. You can erase from your own consciousness anything that you will take the time to do by pouring into it opposite thoughts. That opposite thought meets this other thought and neutralizes it. It erases it. You know when you speak that word that the other thing is not; and because you know that it is not, it will not be. You have to get a consistent and positive mental attitude in the truth. It is not enough to say God loves me. That is all right. That is true always, but God has equipped us with ability to do what we want to do.

Suppose a man is in business and is actively engaged. Suppose he has several places of business. All this business radiates from his one consciousness. Mind knows this and Mind knows everything. All of this business comes together in one point. His thought goes out to every one of those places. If there is the slightest doubt in mind, let him say that this word is one and is manifested there. Let him recognize that he is dealing with a receptive, neutral, creative, plastic, deductive power which accepts everything at fact value. Suppose in some of these places of business there has arisen doubt; then he should think of that one thing as above stated until that feeling of doubt is gone.

Then comes the question: "How far can you hold up another person?" You can't hold up anybody. A practitioner directs toward another person a certain force or creative power, and it will work. There is something right here that responds to everybody's thought. You can direct it to somebody else if the subjective state of the consciousness of that person does not meanwhile become changed. You must instruct people that they themselves are definite concrete people in Mind, and that every thought that they think has a certain amount of power. What your treatment does is to straighten out their consciousness to give them a different outlook on life, a different viewpoint; and as their inner thought force expresses itself, they begin to realize the universality of itself.

A Treatment to Realize Our Own Ability and Power and Consciousness in the Truth

Think along the lines of perfect peace. Infinite peace which is within us. Which is our life, which is God. We know that there is perfect God, perfect human and perfect being. We know that this great mind within us, and in which we live, is conscious of us and that we are conscious of it. It is the source of all substance and supply; and it is that within each one of us which recognizes this one mind in which we live as the great limitless principle of being. We know form, which is effect, is subject entirely to our inner consciousness which is knowledge of the truth, which is cause. This word which we speak casts out of our concept any belief or suggestion of thought or image of limitation, in everything that calls itself limitation or want or lack or poverty. Everything which calls itself negative this word hereby erases from within us. This word hereby frees us from it and allows a perfect flow of instinctive and complete life and truth and love to flow through us into expression; and so this word knows within us, and Mind within us knows, and knows that it knows and we know that this self-recognition enters every human concept of being, lifts us out of our present environment into the limitless possibilities and opportunities which are forever flowing through us; and we see and feel every good thing as perfect things within our own concept. Every desire, every good accomplished we feel and know that we are one with every living soul, every idea, with every perfect and big thing in the universe. We know that omniscience dissolves every sense of limitation; and we awake in the realization of the eternal I Am that I Am.

The Joy of Living

It goes without saying that this philosophy which I am teaching and this method is not necessarily a religion. Do not think of it as such unless you care to think of it in that way. The question often comes up to those who are religiously inclined: "What is the personality of God and the meaning of Christ?" Perhaps it will be a help in explaining to people what we mean by God. We have taken away from the limits of God through a process of reasoning which proves that God knows nothing outside itself and that every act that takes place is some act taking place in your mind.

There are two schools of philosophy. The first is that which denies the mottled expressions and existence. Everything is unreal, a dream and an illusion. Christian Science does not deny the body, neither does it deny any organ in the body. It denies a material existence, as does everyone who thinks deeply. That thought is correct. It is not the truth to say that you have no body. It is the truth to say you have no material body as by material you mean something which is not spiritual. We have a body. It is not right to say you have no heart; therefore, you can have no heart trouble. It is correct to say you have no material heart which can hurt; and in actuality there is but one heart and that one heart beats in each one of us.

There are schools of thought cropping up which say you have no heart; and that there is no matter; therefore, nothing is the matter. This is correct if you know what you are talking about. It is not true that everything is a dream or an illusion. For instance, I make a mark. Now there is actually a mark made there. Every one of you sees that mark and if ten million people would pass through here, each one of them would see that mark, but that mark did not exist unless you would see it. If you know it is there, it does exist. So is everything in reality existent as we perceive it and it is not existent if we don't. You are not getting anywhere in religion or philosophy or science by denying that which appears to be.

Suppose a woman cut her finger. The illusion is in what one calls pain. If you would separate the finger from the body, the finger wouldn't hurt. You hurt through the finger. You love through the heart. Love and fear directly affect the heart. We think through the brain. The brain does not think but our mind, sending out thought, causes it to move to the brain which passes to subjective deduction and in this way habits are formed.

We say we lose our memory. No memory can be lost. Nobody ever lost their memory. That is an illusion. It is the truth that people seem not to remember. It is a fact that it is impossible to forget unless we erase that remembrance by a direct opposite thought. When you say you lose your memory, what you mean is that the channel seems to have stopped.

Of the two schools of thought along these lines, the one is the extreme idealistic school which seeks to recognize an inside without an outside. This is impossible. What I mean by inside is consciousness. What I mean by consciousness is the power to know, self-knowing.

There must be an inside or consciousness; that is proven by reason of the fact that I am conscious. There cannot be consciousness without self-consciousness. I am here, but how would I know I was here unless I know that I am here? Since I know that I am here, it is self-knowing. The spirit is the power that knows itself. Since it is conscious, it inevitably follows that it is self-conscious; since it is self-conscious, it is self-recognition, to involved movement. Since it is involved movement, it has got to be evolved movement. It cannot be self-conscious without an expression. It follows inevitably that neither could there be an outside without an inside. The outside and the inside are one; but it is to the inside of the pure ideas that we turn as metaphysicians and recognize that these ideas exist in totality, which is the cause of everything and which is the actor through everything. It is a fact that there exists for me in life nothing but what I see. That is true. It is also a fact that the things I do not see nonetheless exist. You must always be able to turn within and decide for yourself whether you are dealing with the true philosophy or false beliefs. Principle is dependent upon nothing but itself. Principle never denies itself and never contradicts itself. Have this as your principle: There is one Infinite Mind from which everything comes. Everything that is, is an act of your Infinite Mind within itself, through the individual of cosmic world, and your definite concept produces a form which is manifest in substance and is a physical manifestation of what we call matter. Anything that does not measure up to that is a false philosophy. That is not true merely because I am saying it is true. It is true by a process of reasoning which denies everything that is untrue. It will never be necessary for you to deny human experience in order to establish and maintain unity changeless and perfect.

You will never have to deny anything; all you have to do is to say that the illusion is in the concept of the thing and not in the thing.

God is the very essence of personality. Cause and effect are one and so the very recognition of our own personality must proclaim the Infinite personalness of that being or life which is the source of that which we are. Instead of losing a sense of a personal God, you will actually gain a sense of one.

As to the meaning of Christ, the cross, and crucifixion, these are all things that orthodox people wonder about. Let me say that the meaning of Christ to you and to me means this: For some reason, a man appeared. He taught baptism which was immersion going down and under and not sprinkling. They were immersed in Spirit. Here appeared a man who had studied the occult mysteries which had been brought down from the time of Moses and before the time of Moses. We do not know when knowledge began, but we do know that knowledge exists in the Infinite Mind. Knowledge was not new when Moses was young. "I am that I am" had been written over the old Egyptian temples for centuries. So here appeared a man who understood. Now I don't know how he understood. There is no question but what such a man was and understood. Jesus, the man, became Christ the idea of God's sonship, not only begotten son of God, but the son begotten of the only God. Jesus did not say: "Behold I am he." He said: "Behold, I am and unless ye believe that I am, ye shall perish." He always spoke of the one universal consciousness embodied through himself; the idea of the personal son-ship is the Christ. As the human consciousness comprehends more and more the cosmic, as more spirit let itself down through this man Jesus, Jesus gave way to the Christ of the cosmic mind.

I'll explain how it is that Christ was crucified. As the recognition of the meaning of life dawned upon this man's consciousness, there came to him the ambition not to become king. He had one ambition in being an example that would prove to the world for all time the meaning of God. He never made a sacrifice. He never sacrificed a thing. He gave of himself. Every time you put your hand out to help your fellow human, God is giving up of itself but not sacrificing. It was giving and not sacrifice and we have mistaken the greatest lessons of service and made a morbidity out of it. It caused this man to go to the very limit to show the complete givingness of the Spirit. The meanest suggestion which has appeared in race consciousness was the crucifixion of Jesus. It is true that God was crucified, that Christ was crucified. It was not a sacrifice nor an atonement but an at-one-ment. That is all the theology that we need to know. God was crucified in Christ by giving of himself upon the cross to prove the love of God to God. All of God exists at any point within God because of indivisibility. If you understand omnipresent, unity, receptivity and immutability, you have totality.

Herein is the crucifixion of Jesus different from that of any other human who ever lived. Every other martyr was compelled to be a martyr. Jesus crucified himself. He said: "The time is come and I am going through this ordeal to prove the principle I am teaching." He came nearer the cosmic understanding of life than anybody there is and he is truly the savior of the world. Take out of it any sense of morbidity. There was nothing to weep over in the life of Jesus. We have records of Jesus being at parties and feasts and weddings and talking with people more than we have records of his praying anywhere, because he was human.

Question: What is sin?

Ernest Holmes: There is no sin. There is a mistake and a consequence. It does not contradict anything. Every act bears its inevitable consequence.

Every act in life is normal. Get over any idea of any attempt at being abnormal. It will never get you anywhere. It will never prove to you anything on earth. Eat what you want, drink what you want to drink. Feel perfectly free. You will evolve power. We camouflage and make ourselves into hypocrites and then wonder what is wrong. It is no fault but ignorance. Live as you feel and desire. As our desire admits more and more of this Spirit, we will make fewer mistakes. Let everything out.

Question: What is chemicalization in healing?

Ernest Holmes: Disease is an image of thought held in mind, or a knot tied in mind until it appears in the body or externalizes. Now we have diseases and get over them physically speaking but the subjective remembrance of them remains in consciousness. When a treatment is given, the practitioner speaks a word in mind which is intelligence, the word, the law, the thing. Here is the word. Here is the practitioner and speaks the word in a receptive, creative, neutral medium which is deductive only. So the practitioner speaks the word which vibrates, moves and forms and produces the thing. What else could the practitioner do but speak the word? Nothing else. Metaphysical practitioners will not manipulate. They will not hold their hands on the person anywhere. That is nothing but a belief that physical contact is causation. This man is sick because there is a false image of thought there. That does not mean an unreal image. It is very evident that physical healing has not healed him. It has cured but it did not heal. Surgery is a science. There is nothing wrong with it. If I believed medicine would do a patient any good, I would say that he have some. Don't argue with the patient.

When you talk to your patients, they receive an objective word. So in your case the word is working both ways and it begins to act upon the thought forms underlying the disease. That is all we are treating. We don't fear disease as a condition or material thing but only as an idea, and upon that one idea you neutralize another idea. The word is spoken and it stirs up and casts out and that is chemicalization. In the process of transformation of thoughts no discordant action can take place. Let us know that that which we call subjectivity and subjective mind, instead of being a separate subjective mind, is simply our consciousness in universal subjectivity. What Christian Science calls the consciousness, what we call the subjective conscious mind, and that which the Bible calls our soul all mean the same thing. All disease is an image of thought held in mind until it appears in the body. All conditions of poverty are as much disease as tuberculosis. The disease is that we are speaking the word out into mind which says, "I am poor" or "I am sick," and mind has no alternative.

Everything in the universe exists by reason of itself and without any excuse for being. Life is. Nothing made it. It is. There is nothing beyond the absolute. There is nothing more than God. God is not an effect but is cause. As water reaches its own level by virtue of its own weight, so is the law of life. It is adequate to complete itself, and that is the point which we fail to get when we fail to recognize an infinite neutral principle. If you are sure you understand it forever and it actually gets into your mind as a concept, there is no question about demonstrations being made.

Question: Does it depend on the consciousness of the patient?

Ernest Holmes: When you are dealing with a patient, another volition, two self-wills must be taken into account. It is possible for a patient to hinder in healing. But practitioners never think of their patients, only in what they say: "I am treating so and so." You are not personally responsible for the healing of your patient. If you are responsible and you get to thinking "I wonder if it is working," you are sending out another stream of thought which will neutralize the first one which was sent out.

When one gives a treatment, most everyone defeats the very purpose that they intend to execute. While they are sitting there, they are desiring and doubting and fearing. Then you get an idea into your mind that you are speaking right forth into principle. When we make a demonstration, we must make up our mind that we will accept everything that comes with it. Law pays in full and sometimes with a universal plus. That means this: As I get up here in mind and send forth a thought, it will be just as I think. When it is manifested, it will be the same thing. Things are just as we make them.

At all times a practitioner must have a vision of peace. Nothing will give you a vision of peace but poise, and poise will come only as you recognize what you are and who you are, and the poise with a consciousness of that power which we are using, which itself is the actor which gives birth to peace. Peace, poise, and power make a real thing.

We must demonstrate prosperity just as we will heal disease. It comes out of the same source, one principle, one consciousness, one universal substance. Intelligence, substance, and form. Intelligence is the only cause there is. Nothing else, *nothing*. If you think straight, you will demonstrate straight. There is no limitation imposed upon us by the Infinite. Neither is the Infinite limited when we appear to be limited. If you have sense, you can do anything.

You can demonstrate. Heaven is lost simply for want of an idea. Health appears to be lacking for want of an idea. Unhappiness is a lack of an idea. Peace is lacking because we have not the idea of peace. Unearth this thing that hinders. Fundamentally every one of these false concepts is premised from one point of view. It is a belief in duality. It gives birth to a belief in evil and the devil. We have got to treat ourselves in ourselves. It is true that if I could succeed in erasing an image or disease within me as far as I am concerned, there would be no sickness. I am helping to heal the world.

I once had a consciousness that money was hard to get. I wanted to hang on to it. Everything I saw proved it. I thought if a person wanted to make money he should work like the devil and not waste a cent. That is only an idea. It is now a fact that I don't know that there is any poverty. It is no longer a part of my consciousness. I spend what I want to spend when I want to spend it. When you get the idea of the thing that you want done, speak right out into Mind and *Mind does it.* Mind is the only actor there is. There is no law but Mind in action. Law is Mind in action. So I just got busy with myself, and one by one I treated myself with every concept of plenty. I said: "There is plenty of money, plenty of opportunity, plenty of friends, plenty of business." You must get rid of that thing that ails you. If we still lack peace, if we lack prosperity, something ails us. It is because we are seeing falsely. That is all.

You can't beat intelligence at its own game. It is the very constitution of being itself. Equalize everything in your own consciousness. If half the time that people spend in reading the newspapers would be spent upon realizing peace and power and plenty, you would all be saved. Realize that there is plenty for all. God will give you what you will take. The seed which falls to the ground will bear fruit. The seed that does not fall to the ground will not bear fruit. If you are still poor and sick six months from now, don't discontinue in your work but say: "I will work at the principle." You will feel that it is worthwhile to sit down each day and definitely state into Mind just what you want done. Treat every day. Each time you treat, have the full and complete consciousness that it is done. Feel that it is done. While you treat, say that it is done. Don't feel you have to have another treatment. When the subjective consciousness immerses with the objective word, a demonstration is done.

A treatment is the process of convincing yourself of the truth of what you say. It is nothing else. When you are self-convinced, then you have set forth into Mind the power that does everything. Depend upon principle absolutely. Right here is the Mind that everything came from, the substance, and it is the stuff out of which everything came. Songs, inventions, anything and every-thing, right here it is. It came forth into expression by intelligence and nothing else. Don't limit this thing. Grow big inside. Get over the little thoughts, the little concepts, and comprehend more. Conceive of more than what it is. Say it, feel it inside, and know it. Treat until you do know it and it will be. That is the way to do treatment. It will never come to a stopping point. Much gathers more. Learn to distinguish between personality and principle. Principle is changeless reality. That which we call principle is the infinite through which this limitless thing operates and can only operate for the individual through the individual. Principle is not bound by the form it takes. It is forever free. Principle fills you and surges around you and through you. When you recognize that you are depending on principle, you become self-educated to the real-ization of your own ability to use it. There is no one who has a better understanding than you have right now. There are people who believe more about it because they have practiced it more. There is no one who knows. What more can we say than that it is?

Don't get mixed up. Don't feel that principle is bound by precedent. Principle is never limited to the form that it takes.

Treatment

Take a treatment for the recognition of ourselves as Infinite in our being. Now we are at peace; we are at peace with all the universe of perfect life. Within and without we feel this one perfect divine consciousness of being. "I am, I am, I am." We recognize the law of mind which is the activity of spirit within us as supremely governing every activity of our life and manifesting into the expression of complete freedom, health of body, prosperity of circumstances, satisfaction and peace to our soul. And so this word which we express which is the presence and the power and the activity of almightiness through us dissolves within us every concept of imperfection. Erase every belief in limitation, bondage, want, or lack. It uproots every idea of disease or pain or suffering or fear and frees us, liberating us into the great sweep of universal recognition wherein I am that I am. So be it.

Psychic Phenomena or
Phenomena of the Soul

It is a thing that is misunderstood, and people are superstitious about it. Get the book called *The Unknown Guest* and read it. Also Hudson's *Law of Psychic Phenomena* and Judge Troward's *Edinburgh Lectures on Mental Science*. Read especially the chapters on the subjective mind, both individual and universal.†

We are speaking about the infinite when we speak about life. There can be no two infinites because chaos and not cosmos would be the result. There is but one power and that one is indivisible. If that is all that there is, where would you find a line except an imaginary one? Because of indivisibility, unity is a necessity. The higher the concept which one has of this thing, the farther evolved he is. It is indivisible and one, and we are it and it is that which we are. There is no person living who can argue the idealistic philosophy with one who understands it.

---

† Judge Thomas Troward's *Edinburgh Lectures on Mental Science* and Thomas Jay Hudson's *Law of Psychic Phenomena* remain in print. *The Unknown Guest* by Maurice Maeterlinck may be found in used-book stores. —Ed.

Everything is mind, and we trace our life as I told you in the first lesson on healing. We are beyond, out of subjectivity. The soil and everything comes forth from subjectivity beyond the threshold of objectivity or infinite consciousness. Since everything is thought, back of everything is a definite mental image. How long would that mental image exist in mind? It would exist until it was erased, until something neutralized it. Every thought which has ever been created by the mind in us or mind of God exists in this universal subjectivity until it either has fulfilled its purpose or is neutralized by some force opposite it either consciously or unconsciously.

Suppose you sit down in Mind and you say: "There is one common mind in which there are many personalities." There is one thing from which everything comes. Here is the universal flow of subjectivity which wells up in every person's thought unconsciously. If the objective were erased, you would be subject to those thought forces as they flowed through you. The objective is temporarily removed, and they are subjectively coming to the surface.

A medium is one who objectifies subjectivity. Most mediums, in order to objectify subjectivity, have to de-objectify themselves in order to do it, and that is a trance. That means sinking back into subjectivity. In other words, they are self-hypnotizing themselves through auto-suggestion.

A medium is one who is partially or wholly subjective, through some process or another. I have known mediums who could become more or less psychic, which is really subjective mind reading, who could do it at least to a great degree without in any way squelching their own objectivity. The end and aim of evolution is that we are coming to a point where the whole cosmos flows in recognition of self-personality, the unfoldment of the soul. It could be nothing less than that the Father or Spirit should be perfectly manifest through the son or the human, and when that time arrives, it will mean that this whole thing will flow right down to a point and we will be in recognizable touch with an infinite power and knowledge.

A medium is one who, through some process or another, gets rid of personal objectivity. Every person is a psychic, but every person is not a medium. Everybody does not consciously externalize subjectivity. The only difference between a medium and one who is not a medium is that one is able to translate subjective thought into consciousness and the other is not. There is in your consciousness the subjective remembrance of everything that has ever happened to you and everything that has been handed down to you. It is remarkable how far you can trace this thing up.

A medium says: "Your grandmother's name was Louise Anna." You say: "Sure enough." She sees Louise. But how does she see Louise? Because it is in your subjective remembrance of a definite image. The medium goes on and describes her. Then she will get you so far, and it is but a step to anything. She will say: "You are thinking of signing some papers." It is right in your mind too. By that time you are ready for anything in the world. So people get led astray.

I know of a natural medium. She has always been so. She doesn't have to do a thing. She often tells me many wonderful things. For instance, I would say to her: "Tell me about the people back in Boston." And she would call them by name and tell me what they were doing. How did she get that? They are connected up with me through a sympathetic vibration. Then she connects up with me.

It is the consciousness of people that we like and not their looks. Some of your best friends are more homely than you are. It is not their face and form. It is them. The mental atmosphere which everybody surrounds themselves with extends and is known occultly as an aura. An aura is the result of a subjective consciousness. It varies in size and color. It changes color as a person's mentality changes. If one becomes very angry, it is filled with lightning. If you could see two very angry people mentally colliding, you would see sparks. You see that these things are not unreal. You can see how messages might be transmitted from one to another.

Practically everybody on earth is hypnotized or mesmerized not consciously but unconsciously, through the suggestions of those who surround them. The more positive mentality is dominating them. A person who is positive breaks precedence. These people are leaders in politics and religion and other things. It is to these people who have broken the bond of hypnotism unconsciously that we owe the progress of the world.

Question: Do we or do we not converse with the dead? Do they seem to have passed out?

Ernest Holmes: When a person departs from this life, the thing that goes is mind. It is not matter. They have left their body behind. Most people, in order to communicate with the dead, do it through a medium. I don't believe in people communicating with the dead. I do believe that we are more or less influenced by those who have passed out, especially if we desire to think so. But I do not desire to. You go to a medium and you sit with her and she begins to communicate to you a message from a departed soul. That departed soul is purely mental. You also are purely mental. You are just as mental as it is. If you are getting a message from it, you are getting a message from a consciousness which is nothing more or less than that which is your consciousness. What reason have you to say that you are getting a message from the dead? For instance, I

go to a séance. What reason have I got to suppose that their rap-
pings are the result of a departed soul when I am there with my
subjectivity? We are directly influenced by those who have passed
out because Mind is one. You are in subjectivity common with
everyone who passed out.

Spirit of Prophecy

You go to a psychic, and she will say: "You are going to do such
and such a thing." A friend of mine went to a psychic, and the psychic said: "In six months from now your head bookkeeper will
blow his brains out, and the reason is that he has been taking
money, and he can't hide it any longer." My friend said: "That is
impossible." But in six months it was just exactly as she had prophesied, and it almost convinced this man. This medium did see this
thing. It is a spirit of prophecy, but it is not what people think it
is. For instance, I stand up here and throw a ball at that window.
You who are looking at it are purely subjective. Subjective means
deductive. The subjective deductive consciousness is instantaneous
in its conclusion because it does not have to analyze. Great writers
always write subjectively. You look at this ball and say: "That window is going to be broken in a minute." Your subjective deductive
consciousness had come to the conclusion as to just when that
thing would happen. Then in a minute your prophecy would come
true. We would say that it is the spirit of prophecy. A psychic reads
the subjective tendency or acceptance, and that is all the prophecy
there is in the mind. It is a fact that in our subjectivity now there
are those things which decide what is going to happen to us tomorrow. It is also a fact that they are nothing but a mental picture.
Mediums are all explained from the standpoint of subjectivity,

mind reading, seeing at a distance, et cetera. A medium is one who connects up with the consciousness and can describe it accurately. There are other phenomena such as slate writing or independent voices. These are all subjective.

There are several explanations as to psychic phenomena. Crocker has proven that there is a psychic stuff. For instance, here is a medium sitting on a chair. Here is the table. She is going to tip this table. The medium is balanced on a set of scales. When the table lifts up, she is that much heavier. When the table is pressed down, she is that much lighter. He states that there was a sort of psychic arm which went up under the table and manipulated it. He has scientifically proven this to be true. His theology is spiritualistic. He states that this psychic phenomenon is manipulated by entities. If you stand between the medium and the table, it won't work. Mediums are not normal people.

As to the thought forms or the appearance of thought forms as ghosts, you may discover that these things actually happen. Ghosts are thought forms created for a certain purpose and as soon as that purpose is complied with or the thing for which they are created is done, they disappear and will never return again. That thing proves thought. That is a thought form created by such definite thoughts that it takes real embodiment and form and looks like a person and carries out its purpose and disappears. That proves the reality of our thought as form, as we do not see that our thought in mind is independent of things, and of itself externalizes, and has within itself the power to express itself. All disease is psychic phenomena.

What happens to us? We come out of subjectivity into objectivity at birth. From every obvious viewpoint, we return again into subjectivity. Here are two things that happen: It is theoretical that we pass out of this body. If we pass out in a completely objectified state, we are still conscious. There are only two ways we could pass out. We come into this world and in this world evolve our objectivity, but we bring into this world the seed of that objectivity and personality, else we could not have evolved. Is it not clear that we bring with us the seed of objectivity? We develop that objectivity here; we personify it and choose it. When it dies or goes through the process which we call death, the heart goes back into subjectivity. For instance, ask yourself this question: Does that objectivity which is evolved during life experience, which has the brain for its instrument, does it still function as an objectivity or does it go back into subjectivity? Upon that question hinges the possibility or the probability of what is called physical reincarnation. If we pass out subjectively, we don't mean that we pass out of our individuality. If we passed out in total consciousness, we would be just as we are now. There are many people who do not believe that. Theosophists do not believe it. As we go out subjectively, we swing around that cycle until it brings us right back to a rebirth at the point where we passed out. This would be mechanical, compulsory, and arbitrary to the law. We could not decide any further than ourselves, having no objective to choose from. Within that very teaching also is the teaching that as soon as an individual has evolved, then the wheel of necessity ceases because as soon as we evolve, to the point where the objective maintains itself, there is no longer any law against it. Everyone passes out in totality and keeps right on in straight progression.

Question: When we pass out of this existence, do we have another physical body?

Ernest Holmes: Immortality of the soul means that we are surviving our physical experience carrying with us our individuality, our personality, our remembrance and recognition to know and be known. If you could satisfy your consciousness that such is the case you would certainly feel that you would have ample grounds for believing in immortality. That you should survive your body, that is immortality in a sense. That you should survive your body, that I should survive this body which I have this minute, immortalizes my soul. We prove the immortality of our being. Today we remember; today we talk. A year ago we did the same thing. Fifty years from now we will do the same thing. We survive our bodies, twenty, thirty, fifty, and one hundred years from now. It would be ridiculous to suppose that it would ever stop.

Concentration of thought. When you concentrate your thoughts, that is going into the silence. You are not "going" anywhere; you know that. You simply cease the objective struggle in order that you may subjectively realize that which you clearly realize subjectively becomes a part of the universal swing of causation, which will bring back to your experience the word or condition of that thing which you cognize at the level of its own concept.

Treatment

Forget everything. Forget every sense of struggle or strife and realize peace, perfect peace, and satisfaction. We know there is one perfect life, one limitless love, one eternal God, and we know that that one Mind which is God, being the only Mind there is, is that Mind which we use and we know that no other thought can influence us. We know ourselves to be divine centers in this one perfect Mind, and we know that this word—that this word of truth—erases within us any fear or lack or disease or grief or sense of realization of perfect peace and joy and happiness. Let us each one silently conceive of ourselves as being that which we wish to be. And it is done unto us as we believe and we know that the seed which falls to the ground shall bear fruit of its own kind. So be it.

Some conclusions: We are all immersed in a psychic life. Within this infinite psychic life, or subjective consciousness, there is the possibility and the thought not only of everything that we have ever done but everything that God ever thought. In other words, cosmic purpose. A cosmic purpose is the power of the concept behind the unfoldment of ourselves in everything. It means that all purposes of God and us exist right at the center of your own consciousness. Not only do they exist in this totality as a purpose but in their completion as an accomplishment. The moment you give to deductive consciousness the realization of the end, that is the completion of the unfoldment, of the manifestation of almightiness itself.

You will find that the great truths which have been caught were discerned by individuals who had meditated upon these truths until they had penetrated the cosmic purpose. God did not reward them because of their meditation. There is no such thing as Providence. There could not be such a thing as Providence from the standpoint as it is spoken of. Everything must be law and there is a Providence which is self-assertive and it was not a special act of God but a specialized act of an individual. There is no specialized creation, but we specialize creation. It seems as though the Infinite, having brought us through subjectivity up to a point of self-consciousness, must perceive of its own divine individuality without which no objective individuality could be evolved.

"The Father works until now, and now the son works." This is made clear that mechanical evolution ceased the day that we recognized ourselves as an entity. Everything must be done through us as we discover ourselves and that thing flows through. All knowledge both human and divine exists at the point of your own con-sciousness.

If we could penetrate into subjectivity with clearness, we would have no trouble in diagnosing what troubles us. What we need to do is to analyze out of ourselves, get out of ourselves whatever there is in there that hinders us. I am is the end and aim of the spiritual unfoldment, and it brings the whole cosmic pur-pose to a point of self-consciousness or personified recognition.

How are we to go about it? Suppose there is something you want to know. That is in Mind. When you say "I want to know it," it is announced in Mind and the answer is there. Is that true of anything? In principle, it is true; in practice, it is as true as we make it. People must realize that no matter how infinite the Infinite may be, it can only become to them what it can become through them. We must look at ourselves with our own eyes. If we could open up, clean house mentally, and get out of ourselves everything that ails us, I don't care what the poverty is or the misery is, everything would be allowed because the Infinite cannot refuse anything. Suppose a person wanted to invent a talking machine. There had not been a talking machine before. It is true that everything exists in the Infinite as a potential possibility. It is not true that every-thing exists in the Infinite as a manifest fact. That is clear when you recognize that we ourselves are the unfoldment of that Infinite into higher specialized manifestations. So a person conceived that there could be a talking machine which was carefully worked out in this person's consciousness. There is an answer to your question when you ask it. Before you can speak audibly, the desire creates the thing which produces the culmination of it at once. If we could get out of our consciousness these things that hinder this omniscience from flowing through into objective recognition, we would live a life without effort. The difficulty in getting a psychic reading in order to find out what ails us is this: The psychics deal only with the subjective and in order to make themselves negative to you, must at the same time make themselves negative to all the thought forms surrounding you, and are apt to misinterpret. That is why this method fails. Psychics diagnosing for diseases fail because they get mixed up in this great sweep of thought forms and don't get the thing clear at all. It is a chaotic method.

Suppose you want to know something. You want to know just how to do a certain thing and you don't know how to do it. You impress that upon your consciousness and know that you will be able to do it. Impress it upon your consciousness and the answer you get will be correct. How will we know when we have the right answer? There is no way or reason. You just have to do it until you know. I don't want to give you any formula. That would be useless. I know that formulas aren't good in the healing of disease. They have been tried for fifty years and have failed. Why? Because you are just repeating a bunch of words; anybody can do that. That which works is the consciousness behind the words you speak. Your own practice will teach you sooner or later just how to treat each case.

Suppose you didn't know how to do it. Often in treating I would say that I have said everything that I can think of. The spirit of truth in me directs what I shall say.

The system of psychoanalysis is a definite system—not of healing people because people don't need to be healed—but a definite system of getting out of people the things that ail them. It is absolutely scientific and is the greatest method of mental diagnosis of disease that has ever been evolved by the human mind. That is the principle of the thing: to get out of the individual the true mental correspondent of the disease which they are suffering.

Everything is mind. Poverty is just as much a disease as tuberculosis. There is no limitation to conscious manifestation. There is no stopping place to that which is all. It is not out of place. But the thing that is out of place is in our own inner concept.

In analyzing people, you can very often without much effort go right back and find the mental attitude in their life that hinders the thing from expression. How can we be hindered? Why are we here? The reason is we are losing the impulse or desire or part of that which we call God. There could be no other reason. Imagine Infinite, all, totality. I cannot say imagine God being lonely because that wouldn't express it. If you would get the more subtle idea underlying that statement you would see what I mean. In other words, the Fatherhood, Motherhood of the Infinite can conceive within itself a child in which its whole life is to be poured and from which it is again to receive a spontaneous recognition of itself. Could you imagine that act taking place as a mechanical thing? You couldn't mechanically produce a spontaneous thing. If the Infinite is to impart of itself into the flesh, if God is to become human, God has to come to us through a process. We are evolved mechanically. It *is* not only my theory. It has been held in like opinion by the biggest thinkers on earth.

When we are born from subjectivity, we bring the seed of objectivity with us, *we* experience, we learn, we draw our conclusions. How long this process has been going on no one knows. Its purpose is to bring us up to the recognition of ourselves, as the sons of God, as one with the Father. All these things must be a part of your consciousness when you demonstrate. Why? Because the bigger your thoughts, the bigger you will demonstrate. There is nothing but Mind to move.

Religion is a disease. It has caused more morbidity and more suppression than anything else. Everything is as it is because of what has gone before. I planned to be here. I set in motion power that brought me here. Everything is by law and not by chance. Religion was good but the world is getting over it, just like all other diseases.

The question is often asked: "How did we get this way?" How did the prodigal come to himself? That is the story of our pilgrimage to the lowest cycle and back again. That is all it means. It is the soul going forth to be individualized and returning to be recognized. We see the spectacle of the wandering soul in an infinite mind producing everything that this soul conceives of and ever after the wheel turns and new experiences result and a great recognition comes. That is the reason for our being. We have to be let alone as a wandering soul but never can we wander out because we are always in and we must be in an infinite mind which can produce the activity of our consciousness into objective realities.

The day that personal activity began, compulsory and arbitrary evolution ceased. Jesus comprehended cosmic purposes. He had cleansed himself, not of what the people might call the sins of the world, but of the mistakes of consciousness, and he thereby allowed a complete flow. The spirit of Christ is typified through the individual who understands that the cosmic is greater than its own. Thy will be done always. That is not contradicted. Nothing would be the answer to something if it were contradicted. This is the result of a recognition of a consciousness great enough to conceive that a cosmic consciousness was being enacted through. The opposite or anti-Christ is the recognition of immersion of the psychic life with the cosmic consciousness behind it. We must recognize the purpose through the law. Our karma changes from bondage to freedom.

We come out of subjectivity into objectivity. Where did the subjective get its first objective impulse? Within the mind of the Absolute. Where did we first get our subjectivity? As subjectivity can only deduce, it is apparent to me that because of this we are. We are the personality of God, expressed into what we call objectivity. You can only get out of a thing what is in it. I can conceive of the infinite personality of self-conscious recognition of God as simply imparting of itself. The impulse reproduces itself.

Suppose we pass out objectively and subjectively so called in the complete totality as we now appear to be. It would simply be a continuation. That soul which has clothed itself with a vehicle through which it is expressed would continue to express itself. It is your freedom from responsibility. No human being in the world could produce a buttercup. There are two things true: We either go out just as we are, or we go out just as we are minus what we call our objectivity. We either go out objectively or subjectively. If objectively, we continue as we are. If subjectively, we are, through the cycle of necessity, brought back to a rebirth which is reincarnation. I believe we go on just as we are. I think that all the cycle of necessity must have ceased long ago.

We know that objectively we induce and deduce. We reason two ways. Subjectively we only reason one way. So a legitimate question arises: How did we get this way? This we could reason two ways instead of one. Under a last analysis you will find that good and bad are the same thing. There is no such thing as objective reasoning. It is clear to me that the spirit being self-conscious, self-recognized, self-knowing, is already what we call objective, in that it knows itself. An involved soul is always a worshiper of God. We worship God in everything. For this reason the Christian Scientist thinks on the reflection of God. God is in everything, but God is not only in everything but is more than anything.

Question: What is the meaning of the "Son in the Father"?
Ernest Holmes: God is in us and we are in him. You are the Son and the Father is the Son and the Son is the Father. All that we are is God, yet God is more than all we are.

Question: Do we make our subjective mind?

Ernest Holmes: We create in subjective mind our subjective state of attraction. We do it by belief. We make our own deductive faculties. We are bound in our own suppositions, which bring out the conclusions.

There is no such a thing as a special creation. But let people put themselves into sympathetic vibration with a cosmic purpose and it will work through them. They will be surprised at the thing that will happen to them. That is what it means to rely on principle and not on personality. That is the meaning of reliance on purpose which takes you and takes it unto you.

Since all these things are true, the nearer your consciousness gets to the truth, the more of an actual cosmic sweep it has, the more power it has. One must have the recognition of love coupled with scientific understanding of what we are to do. Disease is the direct result of a specific thought somewhere in your consciousness. Poverty is the direct result of a subjective state of thought which binds us. Your own unfoldment must take place as you yourself declare that you are going to do it. We must take our own life in our own hands; we must be a law unto ourselves. No one gives to ourselves but ourselves. No one takes from us but ourselves. That is as true as God is. If you think these things all out, you will see it in no way denies anything.

Treatment

Take a recognition for the purpose of opening up in our consciousness an avenue through which cosmic purpose is to flow. For the opening up of our consciousness for the realization of instinctive life, a cosmic purpose.

Now we know that as we came out of life and are in life, so we are one with life and we know that this great divine purpose, that instinctive omniscience within us which has brought us up to the point of self-recognition, still knows in us the reason for all things, the purpose underlying all things, and we know that there is nothing in us of fear or doubt or confusion which can hinder the perfect and complete flow of omniscience to the point of our recognition. We are guided and led daily by divine intelligence into everlasting paths of perfect peace wherein the soul recognizes its source and meets itself daily in joyful union, in complete at-oneness. So be it.

Some of the Problems of Life and How We Should View Things

I n the first place, we don't have to think of ourselves as philosophers or scientists or teachers or students or as anything but just that which we are. Forget yourself. Forget your body and find your interest in your work and the things which surround you and you will be healed. Every disease is the result of some inner confusion brought about by some definite selfish mental attitude. There is no question about it. We must learn to forget ourselves. All of our unhappiness, all of our troubles, all of our so-called trials come because we are selfish and for no other reason. It is always so, without fail, without exception. You will say there is no selfishness on my part merely because I loved somebody else so much and wanted what he had. You are selfish in wanting his good. All the trouble in the world is selfishness. There never is any other trouble.

There is a reason why selfishness or self-centeredness produces those things, and it is not a superficial reason. Unity is the basis of all that there is. There is but one God, but one mind, but one spirit, and but one power. When I embody myself in my thoughts selfishly, I am separating myself from that which I think would be my good. You may think this is a very subtle thing and could not be the reason for so much trouble. It is the foundation of most of our troubles. I am unconsciously separating myself from my good. We little understand the subtleness of thought. There is no one who is very far wrong, and all the trouble with any of us is that we are not viewing life from the standpoint of the Absolute—from the standpoint of eternity which does not contradict "now" which we call time. If you can get it into your consciousness that there is nothing existing in the universe which you do not know, you will only know that which you want to see. Here I am speaking to you. If you didn't know that I was here speaking to you, as far as you are concerned I would not be speaking to you. If I did not know that you were sitting there listening to me speak, as far as I am concerned, you would not be sitting there listening. I would not know that you are listening. Then there would not be any of you. Nothing exists beyond the confines of an individual's concept. There is nothing for you that you don't perceive, whether it is good or bad or heaven or hell. And that is all there is to the story of the Absolute. We are as absolute in our nature as God is. We exist at a point just as we have pointed out many times. Potentially, our mind is the truth, the whole truth and nothing but the truth. When you sit down to give a treatment, before you begin, you speak the word that you want manifested, then, realize what it is you are dealing with. This word is the presence and power of the Absolute. As such it cannot be misled or waylaid; cannot doubt itself; God cannot doubt it.

For instance, you read a book; perhaps you will get these notes and read them and study them and be helped by them. You will say that there is much truth in what I have given you. But somebody else will read them and he or she say: "I don't see that in there.

Where did you get all that?"—not recognizing that there is nothing but consciousness, and the word has only the power which consciousness imparts to it.

Every demonstration would be easy if we could get ourselves out of the way. There is no such thing as that thing which you and I appear to be. That doesn't deny our being. That doesn't deny anything. There is no such thing as you and I appear to be, any more than earth and sky meet at the horizon and the sides of the road appear to come together down the street.

We appear to be limited. As a matter of fact, we are so limitless in our nature that the very limitlessness of our nature is compelled to answer the demand of our concept and this very limitation, the truth about disease is that it is the absolute pronouncement of perfect health. You will find in the very law that made you sick the only possible emancipation as you no longer perceive sickness.

You must stop seeing sickness in anybody. There are no sick. In reality there are; for if there were not, you could not heal them. There are people who think that they are sick, and that thought doesn't change anything. It makes a barrier and seems to hinder instinctive life from coming out. You have no body to treat. You must conceive of one heart, and that is always right. It destroys anything that contradicts it. When you have recognized what you are dealing with, this indivisibility, this perfect, this complete, this immutable, this changeless One, that is the thing that is acting. You don't have to act at all. You don't have to make anything happen. If you had to make anything happen, how would you go about it? You couldn't do it; that's all. You don't have to do it. There is no such thing as creation. All there is, is the forming in mind of thought image which is substance itself. Always feel that this word is immutable, changeless, indestructible, eternal, absolute. If you are in doubt, treat yourself until that doubt is gone.

The subtleness of thought whereby you say "I am making my demonstration" hinders the demonstration from being made. Suppose I say: "I am making a demonstration." It implies that you have not made one and one has to be made. It is necessary that you and I shall know there is no demonstration necessary. All we have to do is to know. In order to know, we must rid ourselves of these things within us that say "I don't know." That is all we have to do.

We will say you are the practitioner. You are never treating any condition or any person. You are treating nothing but yourself; nobody but yourself. Remember this. Don't treat people and things. In speaking this word directly, you are simply inducing within yourself a recognition of your desire as apparent in this condition or in this patient; and as you induce within yourself, that is absolute. Know the thing you are dealing with. You are dealing with a power that cannot be denied and it denies nothing. In as far as we perceive it does it unto us. Jesus understood these occult laws and appeared in their midst. You cannot deny the so-called miracles of Jesus. They are natural, normal experiences of one who understood. I can conceive of how these things can be.

You are dealing with immutability. You must know; you must know. That doesn't mean that you are not active—that you have not got to make the truth come true. A demonstration is made when truth gathers its own power together and takes you and lifts you out of your own environment. You will know when that time comes that something definitely points to it and until that time comes, stay where you are so that you will know that you have made a demonstration. I do not consider it a demonstration if we give our treatment and then have to struggle just the same as ever.

I can't see that we have added one thing to our well-being. But I know that principle is immutable and I know that in as far as any individual can actively induce within his consciousness a definite concrete desire of acceptance, that thing is going to be.

Cause and effect are but the two sides of your thought. There is no such thing as cause and effect separated. The prayer is its own answer. Now if that prayer partly believes, there is a tendency to see the thing going; if the next day the whole doubts, then it is wiped out. A form partially appeared and again was erased; that is all. We behold the infinitude of space hung with pictures; that is all there is in the universe.

You should stop thinking of diseases as things in themselves and entities with separate power. Someone will say: "Why must we stop thinking?" If I affirm disease is power, then I have disease because immutability is brought to play. The Infinite has produced that thing which you call tuberculosis or poverty, but because the Infinite is everything and is not confined to the form which it seeks.

It is a fact that the struggle ceases as fast as you can eliminate struggle out of consciousness; the very struggle after the thing is the thing that keeps the thing away from you. If I say in mind "I want a home but it is very hard to get," can you not see that I am thereby creating conditions under which that thing might possibly be presented to me? In dealing with Mind, we are dealing with a neutral, impersonal force that you can't fool. We can fool ourselves. We don't fool ourselves as much as people think we fool ourselves. We can fool other people. In the long run we can fool the world and ourselves, but you cannot cheat principle out of the slightest shadow of your most subtle concept. We throw upon the walls of our experience the shadows of our thoughts and desires. We must either transcend everything that has come before or neutralize it by an opposite state of consciousness.

Don't struggle over anything. If you say there is nothing to struggle over, infinite intelligence is my intelligence; divine love is my love; limitless freedom is my freedom; perfect joy is my gladness; limitless life is my energy; if you speak the whole thing, it will flow through and can only flow through to the degree that we open the way. If you say "I have to make a demonstration," you must get over that idea. When we want a thing, we announce that it is. The demonstration is not for the thing but to satisfy ourselves that the thing is.

We know that principle means we are using the thing that made everything that is made and it is absolute; it will never be denied; it cannot be denied. The only thing that can deny God is God. Suppose you sit down and see on that table there a pile of green, black, and red buttons and they appear to be mixed up. You say, "I want them all separated." You begin to separate them until you see that they are separated. Your mental work is just as definite. You are separating the false from the true. You must induce within yourself that mental attitude and when you have done it, you have made a demonstration. All the devils in hell could not hinder it.

What about repeating the treatment? When the treatment has induced within you this great state of mind, you will not need to treat again for that thing because that thing will be. But if that thing is not in appearance manifest, then you know that you have to keep on treating because the right state of appearance has not been induced. When the day comes that that great mental attitude is induced, the patient is healed. Always give your treatment as though it were finished. Be careful between your treatments that you don't think and wonder if they are working.

The things that hinder us are the personal things. In your work you are dealing with an impersonal principle. It will work for you just as quickly as for anybody else. Recognizing that, you dare to trust this principle as an absolute thing. Dare to speak and know that it is going to be; just know that it is going to be. Know that in your own thought there is a consciousness of love that is radiant and flows out to you all the time. If you do not have this, treat yourself until you get it. Treat yourself until you feel that inner sense of unity with everything and everybody. As an actual experience see it; don't try to fool yourself into trying to think you have it. You must know that since there is but one mind and the greatest impulse of that mind is love, you are love yourself. Speak any word that you know will be the equivalent of what you want. If some other teacher comes and says "Here are some formulas for you," just laugh. No one can put a spontaneous thought in you but yourself.

The diseases which we have, which we must overcome, are not diseases of the body; they are not diseases of environment, but they are diseases of the mind, in the way we think. Human laws are good but largely have failed. I am telling you the mental attitude for you to take. You will observe the law when you understand these things. Human laws are good but have failed. Don't we have laws that no one should kill and yet we have murders every day? If all these things were understood, we would not have to have barred windows or banks or padlocks. No one would want to swear or hate.

I don't care what other people do. Let them do it. Everybody does as they please. If every charitable institution of the earth were wiped out and had never been, the world would be much better off. Did you ever see a charitable institution which ever completed its purpose? Did you ever see a drug that finally healed? None. There is only one way, and that is the way in the mind of the Absolute. Everything is all right; everything, calamity, sickness, fear, disease, death, misery, unhappiness, and loneliness. It is only when we get to view things as they are, as truth sees them, as the absolute knows them to be, that we can master them. When we get to the point, that is the meaning of resist not evil. It is based on logic; always be positive about it; be radical about it. Train yourself to think what you want to think, to feel as you want to feel and place no limitation on principle. Principle is immutable and absolute. The word which you speak is just as powerful as the word of God.

The greatest demonstrations are always made with the most perfect ease. When I say ease I mean we must recognize that everything is right and so long as anything comes up in our consciousness which says that these things are all wrong, then we may know that we are still diseased about that particular thing. If we take with us that realization that everybody is our friend, everything is lovely, everything is perfect, we will find right there the very thing we take with us and there is nothing beyond the bounds of our concept. Mrs. Eddy said: "Mind sees what it believes as clearly as it believes what it sees."

When you sit down to give a treatment, know that the act takes place in the Infinite Mind. This Infinite Mind is the actor and you are the announcer. You are the chooser. You choose to accept what is best and what is not best. We have the right to announce and mind does it unto us. In order that we may always know what is best and choose what is best, always know that divine intelligence knows everything. If I want to know something, I say divine intelligence does impart it to me and shows me what to do.

There is nothing in me that can hinder me, and you will never make mistakes. Nothing guides you but intelligence. I have raised a quarter of a million dollars at one time through just this method.

The trouble with people is that they don't believe it. They cannot enter in because of their unbelief and because they limit the Holy One of Israel. Get still and think: What am I? What is my life? Think straight back to principle until you think of principle with perfect clearness, and when you have done this, the confusion will have gone. You have only got to think. It will direct you. First you ask definitely for direction. Then it will enter your consciousness as a definite thought; then in turn you give it back to thought and it will give it back as you want it. It is the source of every difficulty. It is the absolute you are dealing with and nothing else. You rely upon it because you know it is now. Don't be one of those who hear and don't do. Clear out of your mind everything that contradicts it. This thing is a science because thoughts are things definitely defined. Since that is true, opposite thoughts will neutralize definitely. It means this: If you sit down here and do your work conscientiously, you will get results. The people who do not get results are the people who do not work.

Recognize that a solid piece of steel, by the very pressure of a little light or flame which is intensified without being tense, is cut in two. It is intensified but it is not tense, and by this very presence it knows not that the steel is there; the steel is not there; evidence disappears and it is what we call cut in two. To prove that you are right, when you induce within yourself that mental attitude that knows this person is not sick, you will see that disease is gone. Thoughts are things. You are not healing anybody. You are not treating anybody. You are not doing anything but speaking into Mind what you want Mind to do for you. There is really such a joyous recognition that it brings you to a place of wonderment and realization in your consciousness that is inexpressible. But it is there.

Thoughts are definite things, and thought speaks into Mind and declares for you other things knowing that this word which you speak in Mind does produce this condition. There must be no doubt in your mind.

Question: Does the practitioner get a concept of the thing in his own consciousness or, in other words, what is the reaction on the part of the practitioner?

Ernest Holmes: It is not necessary that the practitioner ought to get any great reaction.

Question: Does the practitioner get a concept or a realization that healing is taking place?

Ernest Holmes: We cannot all get what we might term a spiritual realization. This is not faith healing. We don't demonstrate by faith. We are surrounded by an Infinite Mind which does unto us as we announce.

As to realization: Suppose I sit down here and I want to demonstrate a home, a nice home. Now what do you mean when you say: "I got a definite realization"? There are two ways to get that. One way is this: I might have evolved to a point where I could see I have a home. Very few people do that. I want a home. Suppose I do not have that recognition which we might speak of as a spiritual realization. Here is Mind and here I am. Mind is neutral, deductive, immutable, changeless, complete, infinite, and right at the point of my concept. I reason clearly when I state I have a home. Infinite Mind knows this and receives it and does it unto me. You feel it, visualize it. Infinite Mind does receive it and it is done. There is nothing that can hinder.

The science of self-mastery is the science of being equal to everything that confronts you. There is nothing too great; there is nothing too big; there is no obstruction that you cannot surmount if your concept of the truth is dynamic enough. The truth with which you deal is absolute in every respect, always. All of God, all of truth, all there is, is right there back of your recognition. Every time you begin to give a treatment, keep bringing that back into your remembrance. You won't fail to make a demonstration.

Treatment

Take a brief silence for the recognition in our consciousness that we know we are.

Now as we know there is one perfect living principle, of that one living principle which is in us and is our life, intelligence and mind, substance and power, there is that within us which knows and does not deny, is not afraid but knows that we are dealing with this one Infinite Mind, this limitless divine principle, this eternal good; and there is that within us which knows that it knows and as it speaks of this infinite receptive good, it is done unto us as we believe, goes forth into mind and is embodied and manifest; and we know that our word is one with that almightiness; and we know that every living soul embraced in this limitless intelligence and perfect love is one with all things and people, one with all life and truth and good, and we are at peace. So be it.

Questions
(and Answers)

Question: Will you explain how love and hate are the same? *Ernest Holmes:* Here is love, less love, less love, still less manifestation of love and that is hate. It is like fear and faith. There is no such thing as fear and faith. There is just faith. Here is a positive mental attitude that you got what you want. You call it faith. There is nothing but affirmation in the universe. If I affirm hate, I affirm hate. If I affirm love, I affirm love; that is all there is to it.

Question: There being only one mind in the universe, will you explain how a person can go on after death as an individual? Would not the soul of the spirit, which is infinite mind, blend with the infinite and cease to be individualized?

Ernest Holmes: There is a teaching which is false that there will come a time when the soul will be reabsorbed into the absolute, into the laws of its individuality. Sir Rabindranath Tagore in his *Realization of Life* says the teaching was not originally in the ancient books of wisdom, and explains it this way: "An arrow which loses its mark in the tree retains its individuality even though immersed in the tree."

Question: Is it always necessary to get at the exact cause of the disease?

Ernest Holmes: It is not always necessary. It is always advisable, if possible. One of the chief characteristics of mental healing—or, as it is called, spiritual healing—is the ability to scientifically discern the thought you wish to erase. You don't have to believe that everything is mind simply from the standpoint of a mental scientist. The scientist will tell you that the whole physical universe disappears. Everything in what we call matter in compound is just a certain rate and number and vibrations of this one primordial substance coming out into manifestation in what we call compounding unity or oneness, and directing certain action taking place within itself, and manifesting within itself forms which we call matter or material thing. The only thing which is different in this form is not the ultimate substance that shall come but it is the rate and motion of this substance in vibration in form. Your brain and mine and a piece of wood or a rock are all the ultimate substance vibrating into form. Science has discovered that in the ultimate there is a universal ether existing in a state of perfection and omnipresence through the interspaces of the universe. Science says the thing that sets that in motion is a divine purpose.

A scientist deals only with effect. A philosopher goes back of effect and finds the mental and spiritual cause. Every great philosopher has announced that cause as the word. "In the beginning was the Word and the Word was a God and all things were made by it." So we suppose that in this universe substance and consciousness move. I cannot conceive of a movement with a self-consciousness without it being a self-conscious movement. We find that everything is the result of a self-conscious thought, a word, a vision, an image, all setting in motion a cosmic substance, a concept, which in its turn produces things. That is the explanation of creation which has been given by the wisest of all ages. We are not peculiar people because we believe in these things. We are enlightened because we see them.

This leads to another thing. Since this is true, when we perceive of a buttercup and a mountain, we are perceiving the same ultimate substance brought forth into two different compounds not because of two different substances but by reason of two different concepts. There is nothing but intelligence and substance and form in the universe. That is the basic principle of mental healing. Since the buttercup produces a buttercup, we find a definite concrete idea back of each manifested form.

From the explanation which I have given you, you will perceive that back of every manifestation, there is either one direct thought form or also a thought form not directly or consciously evolved but which would be the result of a certain state of consciousness. It is not that when a man has a cold he sits down and thinks he is going to have a cold; but back of all colds there is confusion and fear. If there were no fear, absolutely no one would have a cold. We know the brains are thought through, the heart is loved through, the eyes are seen through by the soul, or mind, or consciousness, or intelligence.

Within this Infinite Mind, each individual exists not as a separated entity but as a separate entity. We come to a point in universal consciousness which is God and God is our life or spirit. We are not separated from it. Neither is it separated from us but we are separate entities in it. You will perceive that if a practitioner evolves a system whereby he could directly discover the mental cause underlying a certain manifestation, all that he would have to do would be to be self-seen in the disease. Mrs. Eddy said: "Error seen is two-thirds destroyed." Back of all disorders there is a certain complex, or mental knot, which perhaps nine times out of ten, like all of our emotions, is centered on our affection, our loves, which naturally creates the strongest mental vibration. Three of the strongest things or emotions are love, hate, and passion. Within the spirit of love would be the spirit of adoration. You see that it is very important that a healer should scientifically know what he is doing. It differs from faith healing; it is healing through the understanding.

Suppose you couldn't find the exact reason for the disease. That is no sign for discouragement. For instance, take a bottle of impure water. If you are able to turn it all out and get pure water, it is all right. But suppose you can't do it. If you gradually pour pure water in, it must sooner or later transform or transmute until it is pure water.

Question: Why does a practitioner contract disease when treating a patient?

Ernest Holmes: Practitioners may take on the condition of their patients when they put themselves in sympathy with the disease. The disease is subjectivity manifested objectively in the body. I was quite apt to take on conditions temporarily when treating and I discovered that the result was that I was viewing the disease as a thing in itself, as a separate entity, which it is not. You will not be very apt to take on the condition of a patient if you remember that disease is not a thing in itself but simply a state of consciousness, an idea.

There is another reason why a person could take on any condition. Disease is simply a psychic experience. It is subjective. If you sit down with your patient and make your thoughts negative, that is, just sit there with a sort of plastic consciousness, you will be very apt to enter into the mentality. You have an objective consciousness and a subjective consciousness where things come up through you. So if you sit down in mental sympathy with a patient who has a disease, if you deal only in mind and recognize this mind, you are bound to take on any condition which will not come as a definite thought, out of which will result a definite thought force. You will find coming up into you a certain condition. I remember one time years ago taking on a condition like that when I began giving treatments. It was a very painful condition. I thought about it for two or three days and didn't seem to get over it. I treated myself against it. We never treat disease. An individual who recognizes disease in a treatment as a something would be very apt to take it on and would not be apt to heal it. That is why people come out and say there is no disease.

I discovered that thing taking place in myself and I wanted to lift it out. So I came to the conclusion that somewhere I was taking on a condition of some patient, but I did not know of any patient whom I was treating who had that condition. A few days later I received a letter from a friend who had written me asking me for a treatment for that condition. At once when I got that letter, I said: "That thought cannot enter my consciousness," and it was gone. If you can discover thought, it is the chief characteristic of healing always. It is very plain that it could not be otherwise. So that is the way people take on disease. Make it unreal to you, and you will not take it on.

Consciousness will only externalize at its own level, and we cannot set in motion to produce anything beyond our own level of comprehension. We must not wait to treat people until we get good enough or know enough. We will never be able to do it if we do. It can only work as a law of mental equivalents. The man who has never had any money cannot demonstrate a million dollars. He must demonstrate a concept of these things before there is anything within him to produce that thing, and that is the trouble with many people. They must have a concept of the thing they desire to do before there is anything in them to produce that thing.

Question: What makes people dream, and what is the significance of dreams?

Ernest Holmes: There are many things that make a person dream, but there is not always a significance in dream. When you go to sleep, the thing that happens is your objective is quiet. It is not in evidence. Therefore, you exist at the point of subjectivity. If we are troubled and dream, that is an abnormal state. While it may be simply the flowing through of chaotic thoughts and forms, somewhere in our consciousness there is a definite reason for that dream. It is a suppression or fear of something that might be traced back and definitely removed, in which case the individual would cease to have dreams. It is not normal to dream. It is normal to go to bed and to sleep without being disturbed until you awaken. There is no one living who can demonstrate over the necessity of sleep. It is natural and that is the avenue that nature has provided for relaxation. The scientific interpretation of dreams—I mean by that, not necessarily occult symbolically, but thought research and that is science—that is part of the science of psychoanalysis.

Question: Do you consider that disease such as cancer or tumor can be cured by means other than operation?

Ernest Holmes: Yes. What is disease? What is a cancer? For instance, if you were to diagnose the cause of cancer you would nine times out of ten find that you could trace it directly to some form of mental attitude of grief. I came to this conclusion several years ago having had many years experience in healing, and last year while I was in New York a big thing happened. A lady came to my class who was the sister of one of the most prominent clergymen on Fifth Avenue. And her husband was a physician and surgeon. I was invited to their home and came in touch with twenty-five or more clergymen and physicians. I made the statement that I believed nine out of ten of all cancers, especially cancers of the stomach, could be traced to grief. One of the physicians said: "You are absolutely right." I knew I was right, but was glad to have his opinion, however. If they can be traced to an attitude of grief and you can remove the avenue of grief, the cancer will go with it. It is just cause and effect. It cannot be otherwise. I have seen many cancers and tumors healed. There is nothing wrong with operations if they are necessary. Surgery is a science. Medicine is an experiment always. The only trouble about surgery is that doctors get so they like to perform operations and three times out of four when a physician says operate, it is not necessary. As far as healing is concerned, we know we can treat one disease as well as another. The principle of healing is not only in our thought but the medium through which this thought operates. It is a mistake to say I heal or you heal. It heals.

Question: What is the cause of gas forming in the stomach?
Ernest Holmes: It is the result of some kind of fear or suppression. Realize that everything is loosened up with harmony and you can heal it.

Question: I want to have congenial friends, but although I send out love, I am very lonely for I do not meet congenial people. What is the matter?
Ernest Holmes: The reason is "I am very lonely." It is this individual's disease. It is one which everybody has. We don't under-

stand the subtle power of thought. As long as I entertain the thought of being lonely, I am alone, and I am creating thought which makes me alone.

Question: How would you treat for the restoration of the sense of smell?

Ernest Holmes: To know that there was nothing which could obstruct that faculty from operating through me. It cannot be lost. No one would be able or could be able to smell if it were lost. Therefore, it is obstructed. It is like memory; it is not lost but seemingly ceases to function.

Question: What did Christ mean by saying: "Ask everything in my name?"

Ernest Holmes: Christ implies the name of every living soul. The son begotten of the only God.

Question: You said healing was so easy. How do you explain that?

Ernest Holmes: It is easy and yet it is hard. I don't find it hard. It is not like a gift, like a painting which can be cultivated to a certain point. In a certain sense that is true and it is not true in a certain sense. People say they cannot heal because they do not understand that they do not have to heal. I might not be able to sing, yet I enjoy it. I can plant a seed in the ground and the ground will make a plant. That is what healing is. Healing is the recognition that there is a universal mind in which you are immersed which acts on your thought and directs it unto you. Get out of your consciousness that you have got to heal and know that it does it unto you and you speak the word and if the word is definitely thought, you can heal. The thing that tells you you can't is an impersonal thought force. It is a hypnotic suggestion. Let consciousness tell you it is right. Prove that you can by doing it.

Question: Why are geniuses abnormal?

Ernest Holmes: Generally speaking, geniuses are peculiar in many ways. Their subjectivity functions objectively without effort. That is genius which shows that the potential possibility of a genius is latent at the threshold of everyone's consciousness.

Question: How can a person who must spend her time in a sick-room learn to heal or overcome the thought of sickness?

Ernest Holmes: Never treat a sick person. We will not get them well by thinking of them as being sick but thinking of them as well and not sick.

Question: How can we know whom we could trust and whom we could not trust?

Ernest Holmes: If you want to read auras, you would have to be a psychic. It is the result of a mentality and it is an effect. Treat out of yourself any belief that any power in the flesh can tamper with the consciousness. There is only one power in which all thought acts as force and in which every personality lives as an individuality, but there is only one power.

Question: How would you treat for one who is in great pain?

Ernest Holmes: You will realize inner peace for them. Treat yourself first. Realize that you are one with the Infinite Mind. That is all the power there is. You will speak the word and neutralize that thought. Just know that it is. You would say: "There is nothing but peace in the universe, quiet, rest, and I decree and declare that right here in this case." Your word takes its effect. It is perfect freedom and this word recognizes the one perfect mind flowing through you.

To treat for headaches: Treat yourself that you don't have a headache, that your mind is clear, and it will work more easily.

Question: How would you treat yourself for insomnia?

Ernest Holmes: I would know that there is something that made it, a mental disturbance, a fear, a doubt, a confusion, an apprehension, a lack of inner peace, satisfaction, or faith. I would forget the trouble and begin to realize within myself all of the attributes of perfection, of peace, of harmony, of love, and forget the other things. Don't oppose but overcome and it will disappear.

Question: Will you again explain the cross and crucifixion?

Ernest Holmes: The cross has a symbolic meaning, the raising up of the life principle in union with God and human, spiritually and not materially. It was to produce the great suggestion of the realization of God depicted through this man Jesus. Jesus was entirely different from any other man who was a martyr. Every other person became a martyr through compulsion. Jesus might have saved himself. He understood his occult power.

Question: What is your idea of tithing as is often spoken of in the Bible?

Ernest Holmes: I have no definite idea of that. The idea might be developed this way: You believe in this because of the law of cause and effect. As you give, so shall you receive. This takes up the idea of manna which I think we could develop here. It symbolically falls from heaven sustaining itself by its own being. This idea of manna is the realization that God comes direct from spirit. We are not to lay it up or hoard it away because there is always more that next day. The idea of a complete flow is that as this flow comes up into you and through you from Spirit, there must be giving as well as receiving, in order to maintain a perfect balance.

Question: What is the Master Key, and is this teaching along the same lines that you teach?

Ernest Holmes: It may be. It may be part of what I am teaching; if it is, it is the truth, because what I say is true.

Question: Why do you charge for your work? Why do you charge fifty dollars for your course?

Ernest Holmes: I am going to ask another question. Are the ones who have asked these questions asking it for a purpose, or because they hate to pay fifty dollars? I often wonder if they are speaking for themselves or for me. They say salvation is free, but we must get over that idea. It is the biggest false idea in this movement or any that salvation is free. It is free, but no person's time is free. If you were to pay me every cent you have, it couldn't begin to pay me in money for the time I have taken to get what I have. When you ask these questions, always be careful in your own mind of the motive behind them. You get out of life what you put into it.

Question: It is difficult for me to get an impersonal attitude when treating myself. How may this be overcome?

Ernest Holmes: In order to get impersonal and eliminate feeling, sit down and say: "I am treating Mary Jones," then forget yourself. Right there give this treatment impersonally and in mind think it clearly, distinctly, and coherently until you know that the word you speak is the truth about Mary Jones and not yourself.

Question: Kindly state what method to take in getting back money which you had loaned and the parties were unwilling to pay.

Ernest Holmes: You have no right to hypnotize him. You have a right to know that only justice could operate through him and through him to you. Principle is not bound by precedent. Know that you know and mind knows that it knows of your value and worth and brings out that recognition, that realization of life.

Question: How can we get a mental equivalent?

Ernest Holmes: By practice, meditation, thought, study, intelligence, concentration, inspiration, hope, faith, love, prayer, desire, and work; there is no other way. Suppose I had a business which was fair but not good. I wanted to make it better. I must treat myself to induce within myself a consciousness of a still greater activity until there is no longer anything in me which denies that greater activity and until it is very real to me, even before it is objectified.

Question: How is one to protect oneself from psychic vamps?

Ernest Holmes: Most people who have psychic experiences are afraid to mention it, for fear they are thought to be strange. This is not an absurd question but is a question which perhaps everybody might ask; after all, a psychic experience is a condition of the mind. For instance, if I am in a negative state and get into a room where sick people are, I will not feel well when I go out. I have received an impression; that is a psychic experience. It was an unconscious, vague, subtle something which disturbed me and brought to mind that state of feeling that I don't feel well. It might be hypnotism. It is a psychic experience.

Question: What mental treatment would you give for one who has lost a friend?

Ernest Holmes: You should realize for them that the consciousness of the realization of Unity, which is the one mind in every personality, is eternal mind and that there is no separation. As the consciousness cognizes the realization of unity, that sense of loss is supplied with a consciousness of presence and healing takes place.

Question: What is habit?
Ernest Holmes: It is a desire to express something which you feel gives life satisfaction.

Question: What is the cosmic reason?
Ernest Holmes: It is energy, divine urge, or desire or spirit to impress itself. There is a divine mind at the center, the only mind there is.

Question: How would you heal the drug habit or any habit?
Ernest Holmes: We do not have willpower enough to quit the habit. You do not heal through faith. You do not recognize faith healing. There is a law there and you have to charge that law. It is a mental thing. You see mentally just exactly what you want to happen. If you want a person to overcome a habit, you think that thing. Think directly. Do not be chaotic. Renounce all dependent things. Fasting, feasting, or any of the material programs do not bring a person health. You must renounce that this life depends on this body. To renounce the world and all material things is not necessary. Exercise your willpower over the patient through suggestion. Hypnotism is the act of removing the person's objective resistance completely. Suggestion is a mild form of hypnotism. A metaphysician recognizes he has no patient to heal. There is no person here who has a real habit. There is no

person here through whom an impersonal belief is operated in the form of a desire to smoke. Impersonal mental thought force predominates in the mind of the practitioner. Distance has nothing to do with it. Mind is all one. You should realize who you are and what you are. Think until you are the truth. It must come to you. Keep on thinking until you get the one intelligence in recognizing you are the truth. Then think the patient is the same thing. When I begin to give a treatment, I say of the party being treated: "He is the truth, the perfect expression of life, and as such he is immune from any sense of limitation. He is free from illusion. He is perfect in Mind and Spirit. He should recognize that the word which I am now speaking is absolute. This thing which calls itself habit is completely destroyed and the desire is gone and the habit or thing which calls itself habit is annihilated."

Back of every trouble there is a specific cause. There is not a general treatment which can be given which covers them all. Every treatment which is given, every statement that is made, is just that much more which will ultimately free the race. Talking to the patient is much better than mental suggestion; it is more effective. The person must not be negatively inclined. The patient must be very willing to submit to the practitioner's ideas.

Question: What about a mother who wants her drunken son healed and the son works against her?

Ernest Holmes: Go to the healer and let him work through the mother, not directly on the son. He must not see the son or think of him. He must work through the mother. Get her to realize what it means to be patient and always desiring that her son receive her desires. Get her in a receptive mood is all that you can do.

Question: What would happen if two or three people demonstrated for the same thing; say, for instance, for a certain business or a piece of real estate?

Ernest Holmes: If they are doing it simply on what we term the mental plane, the one whose thought is most positive will get the desired object. If a person's mind is not specific, he will make this demonstration but the conditions which come with it will be the outcome of the concept of his mind when he is doing it. It is simply cause and effect working out.

Question: How do you treat for stammering?

Ernest Holmes: Stammering which people have from early childhood is no doubt the result of a suppressed emotion of the child's parents somewhere. It is a subjective tendency inherited which might be traced back to a direct expression of the body of the parents. Recognize perfect freedom. Destroy the belief in inherited troubles. Always be specific. Take into account every broken law. Declare that this word destroys anything. This individual is born of the Spirit. The voice is God and the individual is God; therefore, the person's voice is perfect. God is perfect.

Question: Is it good to affirm "I am Spirit"?

Ernest Holmes: Yes it is. You are the truth. Spirit is truth. Therefore you are Spirit.

Question: Can one cause sickness and accidents to another as well as health and prosperity? If so, is that race suggestion?

Ernest Holmes: Yes. If a person argues in her mind to destroy the other party, that is aggressive maliciousness or mal-practice. There are different kinds of mal-practice. One is mal-aggression, where one individual sits down and destroys, consciously destroys, the good in another. Another is innocent or ignorant practice, or fear thoughts which one exercises over children or loved ones.

Question: What is the source of thought?

Ernest Holmes: The source of thought is consciousness. Thought is not cause; it is effect. Intelligence is cause. First comes consciousness, then thought, then comes the word, then the law, and then the thing. Consciousness is eternal, without beginning and without end.

Question: How do you treat a backward child?

Ernest Holmes: When intelligence does not come out, it is because the physical avenues are not developed to a capacity to allow it to come out. It is the readjustment through those capacities which allows a greater flow of intelligence through it.

Question: What causes varicose veins?

Ernest Holmes: It is lack of circulation. It is caused by mental suppression. Specifically diagnose the individual.

Question: How would you treat for enlarged joints caused by wearing short shoes?

Ernest Holmes: Remove the shoes. You must not violate the laws of nature and expect to be normal. A normal mind will produce a normal activity in the body.

Question: What do you mean by the Word?

Ernest Holmes: The Word is the activity of Intelligence.

Question: How do you treat for great grief over loss of Mother?

Ernest Holmes: Always recognize the unity of mind and recognize that there is always presence in Mind. Never entertain a thought of absence. When you realize this and your consciousness realizes there is no separation, the grief disappears.

You would protect yourself from a mental influence, a false mental influence, by shutting out of your consciousness the belief or thought or acceptance of anything whether in the flesh or out of it. If you entertain that thought, no power can hypnotize you. Psychic thought, hypnotic force, consciously or unconsciously carried out to its ultimate conclusion, produces a hypnotic state. You simply state the word and know that it is done.

Question: There is no name given in Heaven whereby one shall be saved but the name of Jesus Christ, the savior of all. Where are our friends who have passed from us?

Ernest Holmes: Jesus is a man in common with Joshua and Jehoshaphat. Jesus is a name like Ernest or any other name. Christ interpreted does not mean the only begotten son of God but it means the son begotten of the only God. This is an entirely different light. Jesus did not say: "I am he and unless ye believe that I am he, yet shall perish in your sins." He said: "Spirit I am and unless ye believe that *I am* which is God, ye shall perish in your sins." Don't we bring on our mistakes every time we make them? The name of Jesus means the understanding of the nature of Christ. That is our savior. There is one mediator between God and us and that is Christ. The only son begotten of the only God that is worthy of all spiritual recognition of our own nature.

Question: Where do our friends go?

Ernest Holmes: We pass into one mind and one consciousness. We can't get outside of it; therefore, we are in it. According to the laws of mind and attraction, it is conclusive that we don't go any-

where. There are such things as earth-bound spirits. The realization
of that was what first gave rise to the thought of praying people out
of purgatory. It was the realization that as a tree falls, so it must lie.
That which is bound on earth shall be bound in heaven. That which
is loose on earth shall be loose in heaven. Nothing changes. What
you think is what makes you what you are. It is in Mind.

Question: What can be done to make a person who has lost all
desire to live, desire to continue to live?

Ernest Holmes: This means: What should a person do who has
lost all desire to live, lost ambition, faith, vital force? There must
be awakened within a recognition of life. The person needs that.
There are many people just like that. If you are treating, you will
find in your experience that many people who come to you have to
be healed of that very thing. Their disease is a lack of vitality, lack
of animation and energy. Vital force is the cause of a lack of a definite vital interest in something. You will find that if you trace back
the mental cause of this thing, you will be able to get back to a
place in their lives where something died out of their experience.
Scientists interpret effects and the nature of them; a philosopher
discovers the cause of that effect and is, therefore, much greater
than the scientist. People must have awakened within them a desire
to live.

Question: What thoughts cause gallstones, and what is the cure?

Ernest Holmes: One could not definitely say what the cause is. It
might be a combination of thoughts. You will find always in such
cases that there is a fundamental erroneous concept of life itself.
The treatment is simply to know that this word dissolves that
manifestation and removes it and if you know this absolutely, it
will do it.

Question: When did law first come into operation?

Ernest Holmes: No one knows. Law is. Every inquiry into the truth starts with a self-evident premise. I think; therefore, I am. Life is; because I can observe it. We start our inquiry into the truth from that premise. What comes first, the law or the word? Back of law is the law giver. We don't know when law first came into effect. It is a part of the constitution of the being of omnipotence. We create a law relative to our body as fast as we think. Law potentially is universally present. Every soul is a law unto itself and creates a new law.

Question: When a strong emotion occurs at a time when it seemingly cannot be properly expressed, what would you advise one to do?

Ernest Holmes: Probably 75 percent of all disorders are caused by suppressed emotions. The most intense emotions in the race are hate, love, and passion. You can understand that. We find that a large percentage of our trouble is caused by a suppressed passion. We suppress ourselves. It is a thing we should never do. Suppression crowds down a mental impulse and pushes it down in creative mind. It comes up later as a disease. Suppression or grief produces a cancer nine times out of ten. So the thing to do if we have strong emotions and cannot express them is to dissipate them mentally. Recognize it and say it is and there you are. In healing, you discover these causes of suppression by talking to your patient. That is the system of psychoanalysis.

Question: If you want something very badly that you know you should not have, or if you want something belonging to someone else, can you get it?

Ernest Holmes: If you want something you should not have,

right there is a mental conflict. You must straighten that out first. You couldn't have conflict going on and expect to get a harmonious answer. First find out whether you have any right and then stand up for it. If it belongs to someone else, of course you have no right to it. Suppose it was a lady who asked this question and she was in love with another woman's husband. The idea is this: You couldn't treat that woman that she should die. You don't want to do that. What is it that you want? You are after love; you are not after that individual. If you will recognize that it is love you are after and know that love is, there will be somebody to present it to you. We must first know that love is.

On the other hand, we want something and we think we should not have it. You feel that in some peculiar way you glorify God by giving up these things. This is a superstition. God does not suffer. If God suffered, we would suffer throughout eternity. Be sure whether you have a right to it or not. You have a right to the embodiment in some form of that same thing that you behold in someone else.

Question: How was it possible for an emanation from divine perfection to conceive of anything that was less than perfection?

Ernest Holmes: It was not possible; neither did it ever happen. I say God is perfect. Nothing has ever happened which was not perfect. How will I total up this thing? The answer is the answer to the solution of this problem. Suppose this platform is a garden. It is soil. In it I will plant the seeds. Some of the seeds will produce plants which we call poisonous. Some will produce flowers. Some will produce fruits. Some will produce vegetables which are all colors, green, yellow, red, et cetera. Not any of these things are bad. There is only that which is functioning through cosmos and in our life, coming out into expression wherever it is allowed to flow. If I entertain a mental attitude that will produce tuberculosis, it is not bad; it is just an experience.

Suppose that this universe is all that there is in this room. We are in it and we are all the people that there are. Here is water. Every time we think thought it is a definite thing and at once takes form in this water as an icicle. We would have many hundreds of icicles of various sizes and shapes and each one of them would be water, but that would be a form which they enter into. It is just an experience. Imperfection never emanated from perfection. There is no imperfection. There is no evil. There is nothing but that which is, which expresses itself at the level of our concept.

Index

Index

Index

Index